PRAISE FOR SMALL LIST, BIG RESULTS

"This is a true guidebook to grow and serve your audience —intentionally, methodically, and authentically. Having coached thousands of entrepreneurs in launching their business, I find the block of "I don't have a list" often holds them back. Robbie takes you through the details, strategies, and steps to create BIG RESULTS no matter where you start! I love that he also sprinkles in pitfalls to give you a heads-up so you can avoid expensive trial and error mistakes. This is a must-read for any entrepreneur ready to take your business to the next level!"

–Melinda Cohan, founder and CEO of The Coaches Console and author of *The Confident Coach*

"If you're afraid to ask for help, don't want to bother people, and don't seek the support of your network when your plans go awry—you're making life harder than it needs to be. Robbie's book *Small List, Big Results* responds to all the head trash that entrepreneurs deal with by providing clear and compelling mindset shifts that work."

–Jordan Harbinger, host of *The Jordan Harbinger Show*

"*Small List, Big Results* shares a repeatable process to help you achieve bigger dreams and have greater impact. Robbie shares compelling stories to illustrate the benefits of twelve-week sprints, minor goals, and engaging your network. His reinvention story is inspiring!"

–Melissa Smith, Founder & CEO of the Association of Virtual Assistants and author of *Hire the Right Virtual Assistant*

"Robbie applies his exceptional networking skills to show you how to create deeper relationships with a smaller number of people, combined with specific business strategies so that you don't need a big number of people to make a big impact and get big results for yourself."

–Jeffrey Shaw, author of *The Self-Employed Life* and *LINGO*

"I highly recommend Robbie's book for any business owner looking to leverage their contacts. Robbie creates an easy-to-follow framework with actionable steps. His real-life examples make the book relatable."

–Jamie Lieberman, Attorney, Owner, and Founder, Hashtag Legal

"*Small List, Big Results* will help you see where you are as an entrepreneur and, more importantly, where you're going. The book is full of actionable models that you can easily implement to develop your next product, build a following, and even change your relationship to asking for what you need. Each section is jam-packed with specific tools that will help you transform your network and your business, and Robbie takes the time to share his own journey as well as introduce you to the advice of his many mentors. If you find yourself spinning the entrepreneurial wheels, this is the book to give you the traction you need to shift into high gear and move forward."

–Michael Roderick, CEO of Small Pond Enterprises

"What a great read! Practical advice—whether you've been in business for weeks, months, or decades (like myself!). There are so many "nuggets" that resonated, which I know will help me create momentum. Setting quarterly goals, so you can re-engineer if need be, knowing your network is as big as it needs to be (go deep!), and using your minor goals as a fulcrum for your major goals are takeaways that screamed my name. Robbie, you've created a book that will benefit so many and one that I'll keep handy for reminders as time goes by."

–Adrian Miller, President of Adrian Miller Sales Training and Founder of Adrian's Network

"Robbie knows that his greatest resource is his network, and he doesn't mean how many followers he has on social media. *Small List, Big Results* shares specific strategies to turn connections into clients. His "Wake Up Your Network" exercise will help you see the potential within your existing network."

–Michelle Tillis Lederman, author of *The Connectors Advantage* and *The 11 Laws of Likability*

"You know that friend who is always one step ahead of you in figuring stuff out? That's Robbie Samuels. No matter which door you're standing in front of—he's probably already inside. And he's got a party going on. This book is like one of those parties—where Robbie tells fun stories that teach you something while he helps you accomplish your goals."

—Bobbie Carlton, Founder, Innovation Women

SMALL LIST
BIG RESULTS

Launch a Successful Offer
No Matter the Size of Your Email List

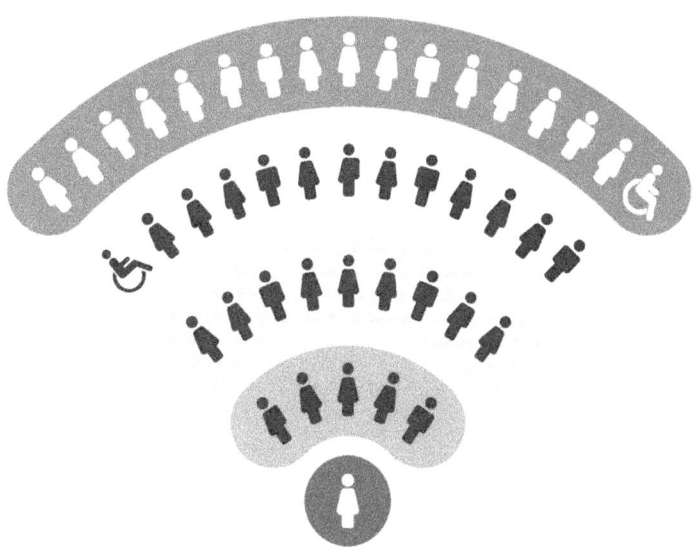

ROBBIE SAMUELS

Movement Publishing
Philadelphia, Pennsylvania

Copyright © 2021 Robbie Samuels

All rights reserved.

The copyright laws of the United States of America protect this book. This book may not be copied or reprinted for commercial gain or profit. The use of short quotations for reviews and other non-commercial use is permitted by copyright law.

The occasional page copying for personal or group study is permitted and encouraged with author attribution. Permission will be granted upon request. For permissions requests, write to Permissions@SmallListBigResults.com.

Quantity Sales. Special discounts are available on quantity purchases by corporations, associations, and other entities. For details, contact Sales@SmallListBigResults.com.

The web addresses referenced in this book were live and correct at the time of the book's publication but may be subject to change.

Edited by Linda Popky
Book design by Jenny Lisk
Cover design by Adam Renvoize

ISBN: 978-1-5136-8936-4

Download the Big Results Toolkit (for FREE)!

READ THIS FIRST

To help you implement the strategies in this book, I've created several resources, including the *Wake Up Your Network* workbook. Download them all at no cost whatsoever in the Big Results Toolkit. It's my gift to you. - *Robbie Samuels*

Go to www.robbiesamuels.com/toolkit to get it!

This book is dedicated to the entrepreneurial women who helped me discover that my ideal clients were entrepreneurial women. Thank you for inviting me on your business growth journeys.

CONTENTS

Preface	xv
Introduction	xvii
PART ONE: MINDSET	1
What's Holding You Back?	1
Your Challenge: What's Holding You Back?	4
Finding the Time	5
Your Challenge: Fire Your Clients	6
My Ideal Clients Found Me	6
Discover Your Ideal Client	11
Your Challenge: Discover Your Ideal Client	16
Get Focused	18
Your Challenge: Get Focused	21
Don't Get Distracted	22
Your Challenge: Don't Get Distracted	23
PART TWO: STACKING YOUR SUCCESSES	25
Overnight Success Ten Years in the Making	26
Getting to the Finish Line	31
Your Challenge: Stacking Your Goals	33
Maximizing Minor Goals	34
The Best-Laid Plans	35
Your Challenge: Switch to Sprints	37
Beware Shiny Objects	37
Going Forward With Intention	40
Your Challenge: Make a Declaration of Intent	40

PART THREE: ENGAGE YOUR NETWORK	43
The Ripple Effect	43
Your Challenge: Be Open To What's Possible	45
Small Bits of Value	45
Your Challenge: Add Small Bits of Value	46
My Pandemic Reinvention	47
Wake Up Your Network	48
Your Challenge: Wake Up Your Network	50
Beware Expert Syndrome	56
Can I Skip Research Calls if I …?	59
Ask Before Building	61
What to Ask	62
The Free Advice Pitfall	64
Setting Up for Success	65
Ready for Research Calls?	66
Getting Started with Research Calls	67
Your Challenge: Schedule fifteen to twenty research calls	69
Pay Attention to Patterns	70
Your Challenge: Analyze the Problem Language	74
What's Your Promise?	76
Test Your Assumptions	78
Your Challenge: Testing Your Promise	79
Making the Ask	80
PART FOUR: TAKING THE LEAP	83
Survey, Survey, Survey	83
What's Next?	85
Slipping When You're Close to the Top	86
Keep Striving to the Next Level	87
Don't Rush To Evergreen	88
Connect with Influencers and Up Level Your Network	89
My Philosophy of Abundance	90

PART FIVE: GETTING SUPPORT	93
Accountability Partner	93
The Power of a Coach	94
Mastermind Groups	96
Personal Board of Directors	99
PART SIX: CONCLUSION	101
Notes	105
Acknowledgments	109
About the Author	113
Resources	117

PREFACE

"I want more, and I want it now."

That in various forms is what I hear over and over from coaching clients and prospects. When I hear it, I know I'm working with my ideal clients.

It wasn't always so easy. For quite a while, I was clueless about who my ideal clients were and how to attract them.

I hired a business coach because I was having trouble filling the second cohort of a group coaching program after a successful pilot a few months earlier. She helped me realize that I was thinking all wrong about who my ideal clients were, and I'd been oblivious to how potential clients were consistently reaching out to me.

That led to a slew of research calls and a complete rebranding of the program, which successfully ran for several years.

Are you struggling to connect with your ideal clients? Don't know where to find them? Not sure how to go from the idea for a new offer (i.e., online course, coaching program, mastermind) to a thriving revenue stream?

This book is for you.

My hope is that you'll see yourself in these stories, take action with the challenges, and discover all the possibilities that will enable you to launch new offers and grow your business.

INTRODUCTION

Your inside voice is shouting that it wants more, but you're not quite sure what exactly that looks like, so you don't shout it aloud. You feel more comfortable sharing a much smaller goal. Perhaps you're thinking about writing a book, launching a podcast, or creating a group coaching program. It's easier to share that than saying you want to earn $250,000 a year, build out a team, and take Fridays off.

Sometimes these smaller goals are bright shiny objects rather than substantive business strategies, derailing you from achieving your desired outcome. Sometimes these are exactly the areas on which you should be focused. How do you know the difference and how do you determine the kind of help you need?

Let me introduce you to Linda, a client of mine who had a successful coaching practice of eighteen years when we started working together. As she neared the age of sixty, Linda became excited about the idea of hosting a podcast. This would give her content to share, the opportunity to network with guests, and greater authority in her field.

Linda knew she needed support for this new endeavor, and she came to me for guidance. What she didn't realize at first was that wanting to host a podcast was indicative of wanting more. She was ready to shift her business and to develop new revenue models that didn't rely on hourly clients. She also wanted to have a bigger impact and spread her message more broadly.

There were a few things holding Linda back. She had never developed a clear niche, nor had she built an engaged email list. With a thriving coaching practice, where was she going to find the time to focus *on* her business and learn all of these new skills?

Under my guidance, over a six-month period, Linda increased her rates by 50% while reducing her client hours by 20%. The result? She began to attract more of the ideal clients who understood the value of what she could offer them. As a bonus, she now had two half-days each week to focus *on* her business.

Perhaps, you've been a speaker or coach for a few years —or, like Linda, for nearly two decades.

You've seen a lot of changes in the way businesses can be run and you wonder if there's an opportunity for you to have the kind of success Linda now enjoys. Some of your friends are starting to talk about retirement and slowing down, but you're revving up to another exciting chapter of your life.

You want more.

You don't have time to waste.

You want to have a bigger impact.

You're unsure how to move from here to there. You foresee many challenges that give you pause and test your resolve to make these changes.

Throughout your life, you've put your needs and dreams on hold to take care of others. Now, it's *your* turn. Turning off old scripts is hard, though, and you may be feeling a bit selfish as you put your needs first.

That's just one of the mental roadblocks you may be facing as you declare your desire to take your business to the next level. That's why the first section of this book is all about **mindset.**

Knowing the steps you need to take and actually taking them is not the same thing.

I've been a professional speaker since 2009. Prior to the pandemic, I was best known for my focus on strategic and inclusive networking. My first paid speaking opportunity was not on that topic, though, it was a fundraising training session for a national board of directors at their DC retreat.

I realized that sharing the steps of how to "make the ask" wasn't going to be enough if these board members felt anxious just thinking about asking for money. So I led them through a quick exercise to help them shift their mindset and become more open to possibilities.

I asked them two questions:

"How do you feel about asking for money or fundraising in general?"

"How do you feel when you're giving money to your favorite charity?"

Generally, the answers to the first question were "I dread it," "I hate it," or "I feel like I'm begging." Answers to the second question were "I feel good," "Great," or "Like I'm making a difference."

Then I asked,

"What's the number one reason people don't give to your organization?"

The answer is, they were never asked to give. That's when I pointed out that if you don't kick yourself out of the way and let the cause talk, you are denying your friends happiness.

This always gets a chuckle, but it also begins to break down the enormous mental barrier that prevents many people from seeing fundraising as a way to create stronger connections between an organization and its supporters.

It's this kind of mindset shift that's necessary before any step-by-step guide can be fully effective.

Whether I'm speaking or coaching about fundraising, networking, or relationship-based business strategies, the first step has always been to address what's holding my client back from reaching their full potential.

What will happen if you don't move past whatever is holding you back?

That's a real question.

If you're comfortable where you are and not able to find the motivation to grow your business to the next level, you will not get more. You won't have a greater impact, and you'll continue to work harder than you need to for every dollar you earn.

There's also the psychological drain of saying you want something to change and then not making any progress. Over time, this erodes self-confidence and makes it even harder to try again.

Don't let that happen this time. This book will help you remove internal and external obstacles so you can leverage your network to discover ideal prospects.

Throughout the book, you'll find sets of challenges. Take the time to go through these steps and you'll start making progress toward your audacious goals.

I'd love to hear what resonates with you in this book and

how you were inspired to take action. Email action@SmallListBigResults.com to share what you discovered was possible through the actions you took. I'm grateful to my book launch team for sharing their amazing progress and I can't wait to hear yours.

PART ONE: MINDSET

If you're like most of the clients with whom I work, you're planning to flip ahead to the section that covers how to make money. The truth is you probably already know several of the business strategies I'm going to be covering in this book, but something has been holding you back from giving them your full attention.

Before you dive into the "how," let's make sure you're ready to get the results you've been dreaming about achieving. Perhaps there's a voice in your head that tells you you're being ridiculous if you think you can charge more? Who are you anyway? Why would anyone think you were an expert?

This inner critic can be debilitating. If you don't address it, you'll never truly embrace the strategies that will help you grow your business.

What's Holding You Back?

Women commonly undervalue their contributions and limit their potential.

Perhaps you've experienced this in your career when it came time to negotiate your salary or ask for a raise. And that was when you truly *did know* a lot about a particular issue or skill. You spent decades deepening your expertise in a particular area and yet you still didn't always recognize your own value and contributions.

Now, as an entrepreneur, you're finding yourself in new territory where you're always needing to learn something new. Imposter syndrome, the "collection of feelings of inadequacy that persist despite evident success"[1] looms larger and larger as you navigate a path forward for your business. Of course, you're not starting from scratch and you're not a complete novice. You're calling upon decades of expertise and experience as you provide value to your clients. You are highly qualified and deserve to be paid well for your talents.

Not knowing your own value isn't the only thing holding you back.

All your life you've been developing friendships and relationships with those close to you. As you begin to focus on your own personal development, you may discover this impacts those relationships in ways you may or may not have anticipated.

If you're sixty years old or close to that age, you may find yourself unable to relate to those peers who are consciously slowing down and counting down to retirement. You may not feel fully supported or understood by friends who've known you and loved you for decades. Your social circle may begin to have friends twenty years younger than you who share your interests.

If you're married or in a long-term partnership, you may find yourself questioning long-held beliefs and wanting to redefine the norms of your relationship. This is a time of change, and change has ripple effects on the world around us.

Deep wounds from childhood may surface as you ready yourself to show up differently in the world. Concern for how others will feel about your progress may hold you back from giving it your full effort.

"What's stopping you from sharing your brilliance with the world?"

That was the question I wanted to ask my client, Jeanine.

We'd been discussing the logistics of her pilot program—a one-day seminar—and I'd helped her overcome every objection she threw at me.

We made the RSVP goal smaller.

We figured out a free venue.

We discussed how to survey participants before the event so she could tailor it to their needs.

We talked about how she could also speak to her participants ahead of time so she could build rapport with them and learn more about how she could help them.

We figured out a simplified RSVP process that wouldn't require a lot of technical know-how.

We planned when to send the invitation to her email list and identified who could give her feedback about her event description.

Any and every objection had been addressed.

Yet Jeanine wasn't enthusiastically running forward with her idea—an idea she'd been talking about for months without taking action.

So, I told her a story about Maria, a friend who received a ton of advice about her business from well-meaning colleagues who never stopped to ask what was holding her back from reaching her revenue goals.

Maria had been nearly doubling her business three years in a row and was feeling stuck at her current plateau—not knowing how to break through to the next level.

I congratulated Maria on all of her success and pointed out that she was a smart and savvy businesswoman. If she really wanted to do more, she would be doing it—something was stopping her.

And that's when, with a few tears, she finally shared what that thing was.

Maria was worried about how her insecure husband was going to feel about her making more money than he did.

"Well," I said, "You're not going to commit to the work you need to do until you've addressed this concern. If not, you'll need to redefine what success is and be content with where you are."

After sharing this story, I told Jeanine that it's easy to say, "You just need to do this or that," but helping someone uncover the block that's preventing them from taking action —well, that's a different skill set.

Jeanine took this all in and then shared what, deep down, was holding her back.

It was an old wound. She thought she had let it go but was quickly realizing this was what was causing her to drag her feet.

Your Challenge: What's Holding You Back?

Have you been struggling to move a project forward?

Are you telling yourself a story about how external issues are the reason?

Is that the full story or is there more to it?

If every one of those obstacles was resolved, would you

still be holding back? If so, you need to address this before you can make real progress in your business.

The alternative is to redefine success and stop dragging around this to-do item that you never really intend to complete. That will free up psychic space to work on something to which you're truly committed.

Finding the Time

As you read this book, are you wondering how you'll ever find time to focus on your business?

That's a challenge many of my clients have faced. They're being pulled in several directions, and they haven't always felt like they could carve out time in their schedule to work *on* their business.

Some of my clients are still working in their corporate day jobs while building businesses on the side. Some have had a successful coaching practice and/or speaking business for years, but their full client list isn't leaving any room for the new ventures they want to pursue.

Time is a constraint that we all face. It's a limited, non-renewable resource. Yet, some people seem to get so much more done in a year.

Sure, you can read books that detail time management tactics, but until you deeply commit to the decision to grow your business, you will continue to struggle to find time to work *on* your business instead of always working *in* your business.

Remember Linda—my client who reduced her client hours by 20% and started to charge higher fees?

Reducing her hours and raising her fees meant saying "No" to people who wanted to give her money. She needed to strategically filter every prospective client through a new lens that kept her focused on her priorities. Time is a precious resource, and we all need to more thoughtfully consider what we agree to do because every yes means there's something else we won't have time to do.

To make significant progress, you'll need to create significant time in your schedule on a constant basis. Unfortunately, it takes more than fifteen minutes a day to lead to the amazing outcomes I know you're capable of achieving.

Your Challenge: Fire Your Clients

Review your current client list and rank them in order by how much joy they bring you.

Highlight the bottom third of that list.

Now rank your client list by revenue potential.

Any client that is in the bottom third for revenue potential and highlighted from the previous exercise is NOT your ideal client. The time you spend working with them is making it harder for you to attract your ideal client.

From this list of less-than-ideal clients, select three that you will immediately begin to wrap up.

This will give you a few hours a week to begin to work on new products and projects.

Over time, reduce your client hours by 20% so you can spend that time working on new revenue streams and marketing campaigns.

My Ideal Clients Found Me

This whole talk of ideal clients has long frustrated me because for years I didn't know who those people were. When I left my career to pursue speaking and coaching full-time, I knew the clients with whom I'd been working for the previous 5 years were not the clients I wanted to be working with going forward.

So, I immediately signed up for several online courses to help me grow my business. Each course stated how important it was that I identify my ideal client. The typical exercise proposed in these courses: Think about your favorite clients, the ones you love working with. What are their characteristics? What challenges are they facing?

I was flummoxed. Who are my ideal clients when I'm in a pivot?

If you're in that spot, I feel you. It's OK. You've got to keep trying different things and paying close attention because finding your ideal clients may be more of an "Ohhh" than an "Ah ha!"

As I was going through my process, I joined several Facebook groups formed for participants of the courses I'd purchased. I made a sincere effort to engage on a regular basis in two or three of these groups—including actively trying to meet with members via a Zoom chat.

I mention this because years later after my first book was released, I started to get an answer to this "ideal client" question, and, in retrospect, these groups were a key to unlocking this mystery.

To be honest, though, my ideal clients found ME way before I recognized THEM. I was super dense about this for quite a while. This is why paying attention is so important.

Having launched an Amazon bestseller that reached #1 in three categories and received 150 reviews worldwide the first week, I decided to pilot an online program of some sort. I wasn't sure if it was going to be a course, a mastermind, group coaching, or some format I had yet to discover.

When I told my friend and mentor, best-selling author and international speaker, Dorie Clark,[2] that I was going to pilot an online program. She replied, "You're going to learn a lot, Robbie." Notice that's not advice, that's a prophecy.

Truer words have never been spoken.

Despite a sales page that was written to attract the wrong kind of clients, my ideal clients did show up to be part of my pilot group coaching program. Of course, at that time I didn't yet know they were my ideal clients.

I was aiming for a four-person pilot cohort and I filled that rather easily. Three people knew me personally and knew they could learn from my skills and experience. The fourth person dropped out before the pilot began. In retrospect, she was at least twenty years younger than the other members and didn't have the same sense of urgency around professional development.

My pilot program was a series of Zoom sessions, each with a specific topic related to the focus of the program: strategic networking. Prior to each session, I surveyed the members to better understand what questions they had on each topic. Using this information, I designed content that was highly personalized to the needs of the pilot cohort. After each session, I surveyed them again to understand what they liked about how the session went and what they would suggest doing differently in the future.

Notice that I did not create a program without input from my clients and then try to sell it to them. I didn't invest in expensive video shoots or online software. I created the pilot program outline using my book as a reference.

Having learned a thing or two about what I could offer my clients, I started working on launching the second cohort. I made changes to the sales page, incorporating video testimonials from pilot members.

I still had no sense of who my "ideal clients" were.

Despite 250 people clicking to check out my sales page,

no one clicked to schedule a call with me. Not a single person.

While that was happening, five people (whom I would later realize *were* my ideal clients) reached out for help creating a podcast, launching a book, and developing a business growth strategy.

And I still couldn't see it.

Finally, I realized that all the people who took my pilot and those who reached out for help had this in common:

- I liked working with them.
- I could help them.
- They were all going through a transition in their business (launching a book/podcast, looking to create their first one-to-many product, starting a business after leaving corporate, looking to speak more frequently and on bigger stages, etc.)

And...

They were all entrepreneurial women in their 50s.

When I'm asked why entrepreneurial women in their 50s and beyond are my ideal clients, I usually just say, "They found me." But I know there's more to it than that and I appreciate that they see me as someone whom they can trust and from whom they can learn.

Perhaps it's because one of my very first blog posts and podcast episodes was titled *When Will Women Win the Right to Pockets?*[3] [4]

Seriously, once I recognized this was true, I decided to focus on building a community of my ideal clients. I'd been active in several Facebook groups that were filled with prospective clients, but most had no idea how I could be supporting them. I knew I needed to attract these individuals so they were no longer just Facebook connections, but email subscribers and actively engaging with me.

It was clear that I was becoming known as someone who could help with launching a podcast or a book. I was receiving requests to "pick your brain" a couple of times a month. I'd even started to offer a coaching package around these topics and I'd signed a few new clients.

Quite often, by the second or third coaching session, my clients were no longer asking me detailed technical questions about podcast or book launches but had moved on to asking questions about business growth strategy. It was becoming clearer that what these clients really needed wasn't a podcast launch or book launch coach, but a business growth strategy coach.

This was a profound shift, as I had not considered myself a business growth strategy coach—despite the fact that for over a decade I'd been asked to give business advice. I like helping people. If I know something, I'll share the knowledge in hopes that it will help. For a few years, I'd been testing various strategies for my own business and sharing what I learned by being transparent in these conversations.

I decided that I'd create a free Masterclass series. Each class was an hour-long Zoom session where I shared detailed notes around a specific topic that I knew was of interest to my ideal clients. The first three topics were: *Should I write a book?*, *Should I host a podcast?*, and *Book Launch Strategies*. That was very deliberate, as these were the topics most often requested for those "pick your brain" chats.

After running the idea by a business coach, I jumped right into holding these sessions, weekly for three weeks. At first, I called them video chats. I didn't know what else to call them, but I knew I wanted to share this content and hoped it would attract my ideal clients to my email list.

After I'd hosted two sessions, I realized they should be called Masterclasses because of the value of the content, the preparation I'd done in advance, and the quality of the questions. I rebranded them and made the replays available at www.robbiesamuels.com/masterclass. Each Masterclass included an hour-long video replay and nearly twenty pages of notes. All are available for the "price" of an email address.

After three weeks, I reviewed who had signed up for each session and, in particular, who had signed up for multiple sessions. Then, I reached out to some of those women and also to those who had asked to "pick my brain" around these topics.

And that's how, after months of trying, I easily filled the four spots for my second cohort.

Fittingly, my online program was rebranded The M.O.R.E. Program for Entrepreneurial Women. M.O.R.E stands for **Money, Opportunities, Referrals,** and **Engagement**—what my clients want. M.O.R.E. also stands for **Mindset, Offering value, Relationships,** and **Energy management**—what my clients need.

(So if you want M.O.R.E. of this, you need to do M.O.R.E. of that.)

Discover Your Ideal Client

Now that you've read my story, let's talk about how you can apply these learnings to your own business.

The first thing you should know is that this step is the missing link between having a brilliant idea for your business and building your avatar or ideal customer persona.

I'm calling it a missing link because most courses start with the assumption that you've already discovered who these ideal clients are and you're ready to dive in and start defining their likes and dislikes (Do they drink Starbucks or Dunkin'? Do they listen to audiobooks or read paperbacks?), until you have a perfect idea of who these people are and how to attract more of them.

I know how frustrating it was for me when I was pivoting from the clients I had toward the clients I wanted but couldn't yet define. You may also feel this way if you're still creating your offer/market fit. Many of my clients and colleagues have shared their own frustration and disappointment (often in themselves) that they didn't get a clear picture from these exercises.

Once you've discovered your ideal clients, then you can work towards creating a pilot. In a later chapter, I'll take you through those last steps. For now, we'll focus on how to notice who is already attracted to you and sees you as a resource.

While writing this book, I shared this model with dozens of entrepreneurs and asked for their feedback. That's how I know that the model I'm about to introduce may take some time for you to really understand but can then lead to really great breakthroughs.

We've been so conditioned to design our ideal business in our minds and then look for clients that it's hard to see any other way to go about building a business. While identifying the "sweet spot" of where we should focus our business can be helpful, it requires us to then find a market interested in buying whatever we're selling.

I believe there are already people in your network who are coming to you for advice, support, and services. These people trust you and see you as a resource.

Some may have already paid you for some services, but they don't yet see the other ways you could be working together. Some connect with you around a topic for which you are passionate and very knowledgeable, but the idea of paying you for your assistance never crossed their mind *and* you never asked. Some people come to you because they think you have expertise when it's more of a passion project for you and you're still learning about the topic.

How will you know if these are your ideal clients?

They are your ideal clients if they're willing to pay you for your expertise in an area in which you are passionate—and you know you can help them.

To help you discover your ideal client, I've created this model:

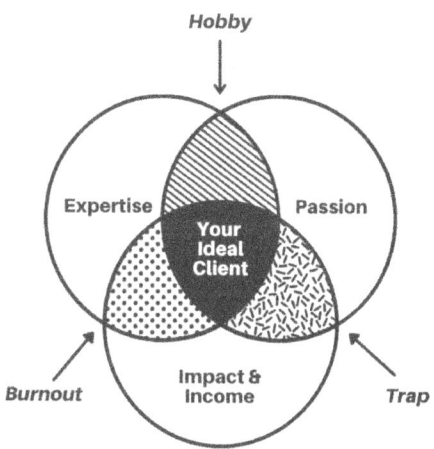

EXPERTISE = You are knowledgeable about the topic.

PASSION = You enjoy speaking about this topic so much that you'd even help for free.

IMPACT & INCOME = You've made money, so it's not just about getting paid. You need to know you can actually help people and have a greater impact. However, you still need to get paid, so both need to be true.

How to use this model to discover whether someone is an ideal client.

Whenever someone comes to you for advice, support, or services ask yourself these questions:

- Do I have the expertise they need?
- Do I have a passion for this?
- Will they pay me for the value I offer?

This exercise will help you discover whether this person is an ideal client or falls into one of the pitfalls.

Pitfalls occur when someone comes to you who is not a perfect fit, but close enough that you go ahead and engage with them.

Pitfall 1: You have the passion and you're being paid, but you don't have quite enough expertise to be able to know you can help them. This is a *trap*.

Let's use an example to illustrate.

You enjoy dabbling in social media. You've been teaching yourself some marketing tips by reading blogs and have had some success with your own posts. Someone approaches you because they're impressed by your results and they would like to hire you to be their social media consultant.

At this point, you need to ask yourself whether this is the direction in which you want your business to grow. If so, then you'll be getting paid to learn more about what it takes to be a social media consultant. If this is a departure from where you want to be heading in your business, then it's a distraction. The opportunity cost will be the projects you need to turn down because you're busy trying to stay a step ahead of this client's needs and deliver value.

Pitfall 2: You have the expertise, can provide value, and you're being paid, but you have no passion for this work. This can easily lead to *burnout*.

This often happens when you're known for a skill, but that's not the direction in which you want your business to grow. From personal experience, I know this pitfall is most likely to happen when you're on the cusp of starting something new and haven't yet gotten a steady stream of clients.

When I left my career to pursue my passion for speaking, I received many offers for work related to the career I was leaving. I'd worked for a nonprofit for a decade, hosting 25 fundraising and donor engagement events a year that raised nearly a million dollars. So it wasn't that surprising that I was approached by other organizations for event planning and fundraising work. I knew the money would be easy to make, but it would keep me from pursuing my passion and would lead quickly to feeling burnt out. Fortunately, I had a supportive spouse so I didn't have to say yes to easy money and managed to avoid this trap.

Pitfall 3: You have the expertise, can help people, and love doing so, but never get paid. This is a *hobby*.

That may seem harsh. It's important to be clear about how you're spending your time. The good news is that with further reflection you may realize that these people are great prospects.

They're coming to you because they see you as a resource. You love the topic they're asking about so much that you're willing to give away your knowledge. You'll need to test out a pilot offer to see if these people would be willing to pay you for the expertise you're offering.

This is great news, because it may lead you to discover a new offering or a new client demographic that you'd been overlooking.

For example, if you're a garden enthusiast known for having a green thumb, you may spend your weekends helping neighbors set up and maintain their gardens. While this could remain a fun hobby, there's also the potential to create a pilot offer to test whether your neighbors (and their network) would be interested in a formal business relationship.

Your Challenge: Discover Your Ideal Client

Get a better understanding of those people who are already attracted to you and may already see you as a resource. Make a list of twelve to twenty people who have come to you for support, advice, or services. This can be a mix of client and non-client connections in your network.

Add three more columns to this list: **Expertise, Passion**, and **Impact & Income**.

For each person listed, think about why they came to you, then answer these questions:

- Did they seek you out for a topic in which you have expertise? If so, write yes in the **Expertise** column.
- Is this a topic you enjoy so much that you would be willing to give away your knowledge? If so, write yes in the **Passion** column.
- Is the value that you offer and the impact you'll deliver so clear that they would be willing to pay you for it? If so, write yes in the **Impact & Income** column.

Then add a fifth column titled **Pitfall.**

- If you only wrote yes in Expertise and Passion, then write **Hobby** in the Pitfall column.
- If you only wrote yes in Passion and Impact & Income, then write **Trap** in the Pitfall column.
- If you only wrote yes in Expertise and Impact & Income, then write **Burnout** in the Pitfall column.

Did you answer yes to all three questions? Congratulations! You've just discovered an ideal client!

It's really important to take into account how others see us. Who has been attracted to your work and often reaches out with questions? In what areas do people consider you an expert? Pay attention to these trends and, when you can, notice the patterns. Within those patterns, you'll find really valuable information that will help you grow your business.

Want to know how others see you? Ask them. Reach out to current and past clients and ask them what it was about working with you that really helped them. What would they say about you if they were to refer you? Then you'll know how you present yourself in the world and whether you need to show up in a different way to attract more of the clients with whom you desire to work.

Later, in Part Three, I'll discuss a structured way to reach out to your network to identify specific problems likely prospects are experiencing. The benefit of doing these research calls is that once you've identified a trend, you can test out your hypothesis by offering a pilot program. You need to get in front of prospective ideal clients to discover what new services to offer or to identify how to improve your current services. You cannot do this in a vacuum.

Get Focused

Maybe it's not your full client load that's keeping you busy. Maybe it's the number of projects you're juggling and those two or three bright shiny objects that seem to jump out at you whenever you try to focus on the next step in your plan.

I see this in my prospective clients all the time. Often, they first come to me not with an idea for a pilot offer that would earn them money but with the desire to host a podcast or write a book. These projects are rarely tied to a business objective and therefore these people keep getting distracted by new project ideas that they dabble in for a bit ("Maybe I should run a mastermind or create a course or run a retreat?"). That means that after months of "working on my book" or "thinking about a podcast," these prospects have not made much progress on any of their projects.

Perhaps you've also thought about writing a book or hosting a podcast. While these projects won't immediately translate into riches and fame, when done well they will set you up for success down the line. Or, as Dorie Clark would say, they make you a "recognized expert."[5]

I speak from experience.

I left my prior career at the very end of 2014 to pursue speaking and coaching as a business.

In 2016, I started a weekly podcast, On the Schmooze.[6] It now has well over 250 episodes.

I published a book in 2017, *Croissants vs. Bagels: Strategic, Effective, and Inclusive Networking at Conferences,*[7] that has over 200 reviews worldwide.

I launched the pilot of my online coaching program in 2017 and ran several additional cohorts in 2018. (This offer has since evolved into a year-long mastermind for entrepreneurs, especially entrepreneurial women over 50, looking for support as they follow the strategies in this book to find an audience for their offers.)

In 2018, I started to better define with whom I wanted to work one-on-one and I created new executive coaching and strategic business growth coaching packages.

I committed to working on my second book—this one—focused on meeting the needs of my ideal clients.

My speaking fees steadily climbed over the years and I started to regularly receive fees that would have seemed impossible just a couple of years earlier.

And, for most of 2018, I was also committed to launching a second podcast about parents who invented a product that solved a problem they experienced as parents.

[sound of a needle scratching across record]

A what? Yes, I was so, so excited about this new show. I am a parent and an entrepreneur and I'm really into the backstory of the products I use with my children.

As I met more people in the world of inventors, I confirmed my suspicion that there would be an audience for this new show and, with effort, several possible revenue opportunities.

It was a "Blue Ocean,"[8] an uncontested market space, and I had visions of helping aspiring parent founders discover each other and find ways to help them along their inventor journey.

I rationalized how this fit with everything else I was doing. My angle wasn't teaching manufacturing and marketing, it was focused on mindset, relationship building, and business growth strategies—just like the rest of my business, and, in particular, my online coaching program.

So, why did I decide to stop pursuing this passion project?

It's a hard thing to admit.

I had an honest conversation with my coach and realized that while I had established a really strong foundation for my business over the previous few years, I didn't have a clear vision for what came next.

It was easier to pursue this fun passion project than to buckle down and do the work to get my business to the "next level."

Letting myself be distracted was a disservice to myself and my clients. I owe it to both of us to do the hard work of creating and iterating programs and services that help them achieve their business goals.

PART ONE: MINDSET

I'm going to do what I would tell any of my clients to do.

Get focused. Get the support needed to achieve greater things. Set audacious goals.

Your Challenge: Get Focused

Are you really close to achieving a big goal, but instead of staying focused and making it across the finish line, you keep finding ways to distract yourself?

You may be fearing success.

Take stock of what's pulling your energy away from achieving your big goal.

Is this a truly great use of your time? Or is it a way to busy yourself with a project that feels more clear and achievable than the murky progress you've been making towards your big goal?

Jon Acuff, author of *Finish: Giving Yourself the Gift of Done*, notes we can easily distract ourselves with what he calls "noble obstacles." He says, "A noble obstacle is a virtuous-sounding reason for not working toward a finish."[9]

Redoing your website could be the exact project on which you should be focusing or it could be a noble obstacle. Working with a coach will help you discern the difference.

What results would you have if you redirected all of that energy back towards your big goal?

Time to have an honest moment with yourself and make a decision.

Don't let your fear of success stop you from achieving great things.

Don't Get Distracted

Following my own advice, I started to make some difficult choices. It started with the decision to NOT host a new podcast about parent inventors. This meant I was recommitting my limited time and energy to my business as a speaker and coach, including hosting my weekly podcast *On the Schmooze*, while being a work-at-home dad.

Quickly, this led me to the realization that I had to let go of many side projects that were not going to help me further my business goals. I enjoyed these activities and had rationalized for over a year why I should keep doing them.

Letting go was not easy.

But then, something happened, and I got really into clearing my metaphorical plate. I got comfortable telling people that I unfortunately needed to step down from this or that activity. I received interesting feedback throughout this process. Several people told me that it was rare to have someone clearly step down and be committed to helping with a smooth transition to the person who would be taking my place. I was able to leave the door open to these opportunities if they align with my priorities in the future.

I also committed myself to NOT buying any more online courses for the year. Like me, you may have signed up for lots of courses that you haven't completed. It seems like every other day I'm given the opportunity to sign up for yet another course to help me build my business. I've learned that signing up for these is another form of a "shiny object," something that distracts if it's not very timely content that is aligned with my goals.

Your Challenge: Don't Get Distracted

Take stock of the commitments you've already made. Are you writing for a blog? Organizing a weekly social? Engaged in committee work?

Make an inventory of the courses for which you've already signed up. In fact, make a Google spreadsheet so you have easy access to log-in pages and bookmark that page for easy access.

Carefully consider your goals for the coming year.

- Is there a new endeavor on which you need to be focusing, such as writing a book?
- Should you add a new dimension to your business offerings?
- Are you spending enough time working *on* your business instead of *in* your business?

Be realistic about how much time these new efforts will take. Make the hard decision to let go of something on your plate to make room for this new project. Clearly communicate your need to make this shift and your willingness to help with the transition. This will help strengthen these relationships even as you step away to focus your energy elsewhere.

Don't let your focus drift when you're invited to buy yet another online course. Remember that list you created. You'll make greater strides to your goal if you choose highly relevant just-in-time learning opportunities rather than getting distracted by just-in-case learning that will not help you move through your current challenges. I'll explain these concepts further in the next section.

PART TWO: STACKING YOUR SUCCESSES

You've made time in your schedule to work *on* your business. Now the question is, "What is it I should be working *on*?"

This question can be a stumbling block that paralyzes you. It's overwhelming to consider the many different ways you can grow your business. You can quickly become inundated with offers by coaches to show you "The Way."

Next thing you know, you've paid for six courses and you're working to be certified in at least two different skills. Despite all of this, you still feel lost and you're not making the progress you need to make quickly enough.

It's hard to know if the project to which you're most drawn is strategically the right next step.

Once you know where to start, you can sequence your goals to create momentum and leverage your limited time. I used this technique of "stacking successes" rather than trying to push three, four, and sometimes five projects forward at the same time.

Overnight Success Ten Years in the Making

As I started to turn my side hustle into a formal business, I was also raising first one and then two young children. Time has never been ample and I've always had to be choosy about where I put my focus.

A year before my first son was born, I left my career to pursue my dream of owning my own business as a professional speaker. At first, I felt unmoored. After having my days clearly defined by endless deadlines, I was the one who had to decide what was a priority and I didn't have a support team to take care of any of the mundane details.

The first six months, I listened to a lot of business podcasts—in particular, to Pat Flynn's *Smart Passive Income*.[1] I learned a great deal from this and I got caught up in all the possibilities.

Every guest shared a new way to earn revenue and they all sounded like great ideas.

There was a breaking point for me. A guest was talking about patenting ideas, hoping one of their patents would be purchased. I stood in my kitchen thinking about how easily I could do this. Then I stopped short.

I'd drifted far from my goal of earning a living as a professional speaker.

That's when I remembered sage advice that had been mentioned more than once on *Smart Passive Income*. It was advice Pat Flynn had received from Jason Van Orden,[2] then the host of *Internet Business Mastery*[3] and currently host of *IMPACT: Amplify & Monetize Your Unique Genius*[4]: "There's a difference between just in case and just in time learning."[5]

I'd been doing a lot of just-in-case learning over the previous six months. It was time to pick a project that would help me take my side hustle to a six-figure business.

Since podcasts had such a big impact on me and I would much rather talk than write, I set the intention to host a weekly podcast. I knew that would require considerable focus and attention—especially since I wanted it to be a high-quality show right out of the gate.

The second project to which I committed was to completely overhaul my website. It had been a few years since I launched the site and it no longer matched how I wanted to be perceived.

The third project was to become a Professional Member of the National Speakers Association (NSA). This required having twenty paid bookings within a twelve-month time period.

I also knew that to be a well-paid professional speaker I needed to write a book (or perhaps two or three), but I didn't add that to the list for that particular year. I knew that if I tried to do too many projects at once, I knew I wouldn't succeed with any of them.

With six months to go before my first son was born, I set to work to make these three projects a reality. I broke down each project into tasks and set goals for each quarter of the year. This allowed me to see the momentum as I completed each one. I could judge for myself whether I was on track or getting distracted.

The first step was to dive into learning about how to host a podcast. This was my main goal for the third quarter of 2015. I began to interview guests at the end of Q3 and into Q4.

In the fourth quarter of that year, my goal was to relaunch my website. I set a hard deadline to have this done before my son was born in mid-December—and I made it. The site was up by the end of November.

It was around that time that I realized I had overshot my

goal of twenty paid bookings. I was on track to have thirty paid bookings my first year without a full-time job.

My main goal for the first quarter of 2016 was to be home with my wife and son. I took slow forward steps in the podcast launch, but I wanted time to adjust to being a family of three.

It wasn't until Q2 that I really shifted the podcast into high gear and set a launch deadline. I wanted to walk into my second National Speakers Association conference having accomplished a major project for my business.

The podcast launch date was the Tuesday before the annual NSA conference—right at the beginning of Q3. A perfect venue for identifying new guests for my show.

Having a podcast up and running with two months' worth of shows recorded meant I could be choosy about who I invited to be on my show.

I was choosy. In the end, I invited twelve people to be interviewed. They were all main stage speakers and/or past presidents of the national association. Some ran million-dollar-plus businesses.

Ten of those interviews took place over the next six months. With their participation, my credibility soared. I was then able to connect with a tier of my network that had previously seemed out of reach.

As I was designing my podcast questions, I kept in mind that I would be writing a book sometime in the future. I included interview questions that invited my guests to share a story that would help illustrate points I would be making in my book.

By the end of 2016, I was getting into a rhythm with my weekly show and was ready to start thinking about the next big project: writing a book.

In early 2017, I set the firm intention to write my book.

I rallied the resources and support I needed to be successful. While I'd made some attempts to write a book previously, this time I didn't waver in my determination.

The stories and quotes that I'd been collecting from my podcast guests were woven into my manuscript—bringing the concepts to life. I went through my list of podcast guests and invited ten of them to write an endorsement for the book. And they all said yes!

This added credibility to my first book. It also gave me a reason to reconnect with my podcast guests—to either tell them they were being featured in my book or to encourage them to write an endorsement.

By mid 2017, my first book was drafted and heading to the editor. Amazing.

The deadline that was driving me? I wanted to walk back into the National Speakers Association conference with another major project completed. I wanted to be an author when I attended the event in July.

I began to learn about the steps of a successful launch—including how much that differs from just hitting publish. I set the intention to have a hundred reviews by my launch date.

To achieve this, I pushed the launch date to the end of July (in mid Q3), two weeks after the conference. As a result, I didn't walk into the event as a published author, but I did arrive with stacks of business cards inviting fellow NSA members to join my 300+ member launch team.

About a month before my first book launch, I realized that the date I was counting down to wasn't the end—it was the beginning.

All through the process of writing, editing, formatting, and publishing that book, I had my eye on the launch date.

That's all I could really think about. But, I wasn't publishing a book just to say I wrote a book.

My book was part of a bigger plan—a strategic plan—for my business. That meant that even though the book had not yet been published, I needed to be thinking through the next steps.

What am I building toward and how will this book serve those goals?

And that's when I started to seriously work on the pilot for my online coaching program, which launched a couple of months later in September 2017. This was the same week I released the print and audio versions of my book.

I'm sharing my story to illustrate how it's possible to keep growing your business to the next level, even when you have limited time. When you stack your successes, time is on your side.

In the first three years after I left my career, I was able to:

- Shift the type of audiences to which I spoke and double my fees.
- Launch a weekly podcast and celebrate reaching 75 episodes.
- Build my authority by writing and launching an Amazon bestseller.
- Expand and diversify my network through strategic relationship-building.
- Pilot an online coaching program that expanded into a six-month program.
- Became "referable" by having a professional website, strong intellectual property (IP), and social proof.

Our second son was born right at the end of those three years. I then became a work-at-home dad and primary caregiver to two little ones.

In the next two years, I coached dozens of entrepreneurs on product/market fit and launched a pilot program with an extremely limited email list, spoke at TEDxBeaconStreet, and became a *Harvard Business Review* contributor.

I built a reputation as a networking expert with a focus on networking at conferences. Then, in March 2020, the world dramatically changed. In-person events evaporated overnight during the COVID-19 pandemic. Suddenly, no one needed my event networking expertise. In fact, there were no live events anywhere in the world. So, what did I do? I reinvented myself and built new six-figure revenue streams around virtual events. I'll share more about my pandemic reinvention in Part 3.

But first let me tell you how to stay focused despite many distractions and challenges.

Getting to the Finish Line

The calendar says September 22. You realize there are only 100 days left until the end of the year. You have several open projects that you've been incrementally moving forward all year, but none are close to completion. You really want to finish the year strong, so you map out a plan to finally wrap up two or three of those projects.

You're motivated, but it's too much, too late to impact the current year.

Too much because you're trying to cram multiple projects into the last quarter, which is already packed with holiday prep, holiday parties, family visits, and traveling.

Too late because you could have worked to completion all

year long instead of using the end of the calendar year as your incentive to kick into high gear. This is why it's important to work to completion on one major project before moving on to another one.

For the first five years after I left my full-time job, I managed this by setting quarterly goals. Each quarter I'd have one major and two minor goals. Minor goals often made major goals easier later in the year. But I knew I couldn't handle more than this while being a primary caregiver.

The benefit of following a quarterly goal structure was that if I ran into trouble with a goal, I knew I was giving it my full effort. I could look at what did/didn't work and make adjustments accordingly.

If I needed to change tactics or abort altogether, I could do so more quickly and get back on track. If I had this same goal with a year-long plan, I'd have some incremental progress and sometimes be stuck without ever knowing if I had ever been on the right track.

This is how I quickly knew my first foray into running a group coaching program wasn't getting the results I wanted. Despite a successful pilot and my best marketing efforts, I wasn't filling the program.

If I hadn't been solely focused on this major goal, it might have lingered on my to-do list all year long without any real progress being made. As I figured out who my ideal clients were, I set up those three Masterclasses to better understand what problems they were facing in their businesses and how I could be serving them.

At the end of that particular quarter, I had finally attracted the right prospects. Within a few weeks, that program was filled. If I hadn't had the goal to fill the program by the end of the quarter, I may not have even realized that the program needed more iterations and rebranding.

The result was a much better offer that resonated with my ideal clients.

Your Challenge: Stacking Your Goals

We often think about resetting our goals at the end of the calendar year, but there's no reason to wait for a new year. You can do this at any time.

Look ahead to the next twelve months. What do you want to accomplish?

Now think about three or four big goals—the ones that will take concerted effort to be successful. These might be:

- Launch a new website
- Write a book
- Create a membership community
- Pilot a multi-day retreat

Consider which of these would be the best foundation for the others to be successful.

That's your first major goal.

Strategically order the remaining goals, considering how content from one might be useful for a later project.

For instance, creating an online course would also give you a head start on a book about the same topic (or vice versa).

Minor goals don't require as much time or effort but are definitely still crucial to the health of your business. These might be:

- Update your website content to reflect changes in your business
- Run a report on your website, then spend time fixing broken links and improving your SEO
- Research ideas for a book and schedule interviews with ideal readers to get their suggestions for what to write about
- Increase the number of subscribers to your email list with a focus on engagement

Have at least one minor goal per quarter and not more than three. Write these all out and you'll have a serious plan to grow your business.

Maximizing Minor Goals

When I first started hosting my podcast, my intention was to write a book about networking, but I wasn't very clear how I was going to frame the problem or what audience might want to read this.

Every other week for the first year of my show, I produced a solo episode where I shared a networking tip or technique. These eight to ten- minute episodes were initially based on blog posts I'd written, but then I began to create a script based on questions I heard from listeners and audience members.

A few months into the show, I realized that many of the questions were centered around how to navigate events. That's when I decided to focus on how to make the most of conference experiences.

Once I made that decision, my minor goal became collecting quotes I could use to illustrate the take-aways in my yet-to-be-written book.

To accomplish this, I added a question to my interviews that elicited either tips or a story about my guest's experience networking at conferences. As I mentioned, these anecdotes were woven into my rough draft and brought the concepts to life.

Even though I wasn't planning to write my book right away, the minor goal of collecting stories and building relationships with influencers set me up for success when I was ready to focus on the major goal of writing my first book.

Leverage your time by using your minor goals to strategically support major goals planned for later in the year.

The Best-Laid Plans

"Man makes plans . . . and God laughs."[6] — **Michael Chabon**

All the goal setting in the world could not have prepared you for the impact of a global pandemic.

Time was really off for over a year. Weekends and weekdays blurred. Annual events that normally would mark the passage of time were canceled or postponed.

For a while, it was hard to forecast plans more than a few weeks or possibly a few months out. Our time horizon became really short.

There was one way, though, that it was clear time had passed. My kids. At the start of the pandemic, they were just over 2 and 4 years old. They grew up so much in 2020. It felt like every three months, they had new skills and new abilities.

The other thing that helped me experience the passage of time was having clear goals. As I had for years, I started 2020 with specific major and minor goals for Q1 and a sense of where I might focus throughout the year.

It is a major understatement to say that all my strategic goals were disrupted in a big way. I had to be much more nimble as I moved through 2020 trying new ways of moving my business forward.

At the end of 2020, I made a decision to alter my quarterly goal-setting strategy. This was a big deal, since quarterly goals had been so helpful in making big strides in my business.

Starting in 2021, I switched from quarterly goals to twelve-week sprints.

On the surface, that sounds very similar, but the key difference is there are now four weeks in between each twelve-week sprint. Before, there was never any point during the year when I wasn't supposed to be laser-focused on a set of goals. There was never any space to figure out what adjustments had to be made to my business strategies because I was always just moving from one quarter to the next.

With this new system, I still create a strategic plan for what I want to accomplish in twelve weeks, and I do my best to push any new ideas to later in the year so I don't get distracted. The magic is that I now have downtime between my twelve-week sprints for reflection and assessment, rest and rejuvenation, learning and growth, and strategic planning.

As my new revenue streams took off in 2020, I knew creating stronger systems and "adulting" my business were going to be a major area of focus for the start of 2021. With that in mind, I hired Mary Williams,[7] founder of Sensible Woo, to be my systems and processes coach. With her help, I've been able to maximize the four weeks in between sprints so I'm focused and ready to go when the next twelve-week sprint begins.

Your Challenge: Switch to Sprints

Ready to try this yourself? This is how I use the downtime in between sprints:

Week 1: Spend time on reflection and assessment to get clear on what happened in the last sprint. How did you do with your sprint goals? What adjustments do you need to make to achieve any that you didn't meet?

Week 2: Focus on rest and rejuvenation. In other words, take time off from work!

Week 3: Remember when I introduced you to just-in-case learning? This is the week to catch up on replays, podcasts, and other content that wasn't highly relevant during the sprint (when you were focused on just-in-time learning).

Week 4: Take what you learned from your assessment, from the downtime, and from all that random but interesting content. Figure out your strategic major and minor goals for the next sprint.

Beware Shiny Objects

Two clients, Linda and Sarah, came to me with the immediate goal of hosting their own podcasts. They each had solid reasons for why they wanted to do this.

Ninety days into a group coaching program, one was well on her way to a podcast launch and the other had decided this was no longer her priority goal.

What factors led to these decisions?

Linda, the client I mentioned earlier, didn't have an engaged email list. She had managed to grow her private coaching practice entirely on word-of-mouth referrals and hadn't developed any kind of community.

Hosting a podcast allows Linda to attract the community of people who would be interested in the groups and programs she's developing over the next year. A weekly show would mean she would have content to share on a regular basis with her broader network, inviting them to connect with her and learn about her offerings.

As she developed the show, Linda had to answer many critical questions about who her ideal listener was. That also led to greater clarity around who would be her ideal clients. This helped Linda be more thoughtful in her client selection, and, as I mentioned, she cut back her client hours by 20% while raising her rates 50% over six months.

The show also brings Linda joy and gives her a focus for the new way she plans to be running her business over the next few years. This is after nearly two decades with a focus on private coaching.

For Linda, hosting a podcast was the right next step. She could see how it would be the foundation for the other major goals on which she planned to work over the next twelve months.

Sarah's situation was different. When she and I initially set up a coaching contract, the sole goal was to learn how to launch a podcast. Quickly, it became evident that the podcast was part of a much larger vision that Sarah had for herself and for her hobby-turned-side-hustle.

Sarah had already launched a small but thriving and increasingly engaged Facebook group around her topic. Under the umbrella of her company, volunteers were hosting events around the country using her well-branded material.

All of this progress happened before and after a full workday at her office. The vision was clear, but the path to get there was a bit murky, as the reality of her limited time hit home.

The true test was whether Sarah could monetize this.

The new goal became engaging and growing her Facebook community—and converting members to her email list. That would give Sarah a better sense of her ideal clients. She could receive feedback from them as she tested different pilot offers over the next year.

If Sarah had stayed with the podcast as her first major goal, this would have drawn her attention away from her Facebook community, while she spent months trying to put together all the moving parts of a podcast launch. Sarah came to realize that while focusing on a podcast she wouldn't also have the bandwidth to maintain an active and engaged Facebook group—which was just starting to attract members at a higher clip.

If Facebook group members aren't interacting in the group, the algorithm will stop showing them group notifications. Once that happens, it's really difficult to pull them back into the group. This means that Sarah would have returned to a dormant Facebook group just a few months later and would have had to start from scratch to build momentum again.

But Sarah really loved the idea of a podcast. She thought her members would enjoy the interviews she'd been planning. My suggestion was to interview these people and share the interviews with just her Facebook group. It would be a wonderful group benefit and a great way to keep attracting members while developing content to repurpose as a podcast or YouTube series in the future. With minimal effort, these interviews could be conducted through Facebook Live, so members could ask questions in the comments.

Going Forward With Intention

I've driven home the point that you can't do everything at once, right? This means at some point; you need to choose. And with that clarity of choice, everything else falls to the wayside.

Suddenly, a path emerges that was obscured until this point. You now have a way forward for growing your business. You know where your focus should be and which projects should come next after this one is completed. You have a strategic plan that will allow you to stack your successes to create momentum and leverage your limited time.

Feels good, doesn't it?

There's one more thing you need to do before you can jump into the work you've so carefully defined. You need to declare your intention.

This is a statement you make to yourself, your accountability partner, and/or your coach. It's the actions you intend to take and the results you intend to see within a specific timeframe.

Your Challenge: Make a Declaration of Intent

Choose. Focus on one audacious goal that you want to achieve this year.

Visualize. If you could wave a magic wand and get the result you want, what would that be?

Be specific. In what timeframe do you plan to accomplish this?

Plan. Create a list of actionable next steps to achieve this result.

Declare. "I'm working on X (project) and will have Y (quantifiable) completed by Z (date)."

Be Accountable. Tell people! Share your audacious goal with your accountability partner, and/or your coach, and/or your mastermind, and/or a family member.

PART THREE: ENGAGE YOUR NETWORK

I know you're excited and probably overflowing with ideas for your new offer. If you're like most experts, you're already building out your idea and getting it ready to sell. If that's the case, you're about to skip a critical step:

Now's the time to talk to likely prospects and get clear on what *they* think is their problem. Then you can build a runway that will make it easier for your offer to be a hit.

If you build your offer in a vacuum without any input from likely prospects, there's a good chance the market won't be that excited when you start pitching that offer.

Even before you have a clear offer in mind, you should be nurturing your network and becoming a trusted resource. Doing so will make it much easier to connect with likely prospects in the future.

The Ripple Effect

Nearly a year after the publication of my first book, *Croissants vs. Bagels: Strategic, Effective, and Inclusive Networking at*

Conferences, a reader sent me a message through my website contact form titled, "You've Changed My Life!" Daryl shared specific ways my book helped him transform his way of thinking:

"Your book inspired me to overcome my anxiety and it gave me the tools to have meaningful conversations."

Daryl then asked if I would make time to be interviewed for a virtual summit he was launching later that summer. Of course, I said yes.

After the interview, I asked for the list of speakers and realized only men were on the list. When I asked if he would like to find entrepreneurial women to share their expertise, Daryl said yes, he'd love introductions. I posted a note in a Facebook community where I'm active, specifically encouraging women in the group to reach out about being interviewed for this virtual summit.

When I looked at the final list of speakers, I noticed that ten out of twenty-three were women and I knew eight of them (As it turns out, the other two were invited by the women I had encouraged to apply!). But the ripple effect of Daryl reaching out to me keeps going. Several of the women finally figured out how to share a lead magnet with the virtual summit attendees in a way that will help them grow their email lists. They'd been meaning to set up this bit of technology, but having a deadline helped them actually get it done.

Of course, all the people who tuned in to this summit benefited from the wisdom that was shared by me and the other speakers. And, I've strengthened my relationship with each of these women by making this connection for them.

All of this value came about because a reader dared to reach out, say thank you, and invite me to participate in his event.

Your Challenge: Be Open To What's Possible

Have you ever thought about reaching out to an influencer in your field because you admire their work and want to say thank you?

Perhaps your life or business has been improved because of a book you read, a podcast you heard, or some other piece of content that someone labored to put out into the world. Do you find yourself holding back from reaching out because you don't want to "bother" others?

Step out of your own way and reach out.

Start by thanking them with some specificity, then make your ask.

The key is don't be attached to the outcome. Be open to what becomes possible.

You never know the ripple effect your actions may have.

Small Bits of Value

"Hold on a sec, we'll have this figured out soon…"

"I don't understand. I know this is possible, but I can't get it to work…"

"I'll try my phone."

"I'm in!"

"Do you hear that echo? Ugh. This isn't working."

"Headphones? Yeah, I can use them. I need to go find them…"

This was the conversation during the first few minutes of several Facebook Live interviews I watched shortly after Facebook made it possible to allow a host to add a guest on-air.

Let's just say the steps to making that a smooth experience were not intuitive.

The technical snafus were so bad that the post accompanying the Facebook Live told replay viewers to skip ahead to minute 4:05 or 9:12 or whenever the interview actually started.

This happened often enough in a private Facebook group that it convinced me to make these interviews easier to set up, since I loved the content that members are sharing.

So, I researched and tested until I figured out the right steps. I then shared these insights in a Facebook post in that private group and in several other Facebook groups where I thought this information would be valuable.

Offering value is often about noticing a problem and being willing to research and test a solution.

Your Challenge: Add Small Bits of Value

Keep your eyes and ears open for small problems that you can help resolve.

If there's something you've figured out to make your life easier, create a tutorial so you can easily share the details.

Create a page on your website filled with resources and referrals so the information is always a few clicks away.

Here's mine: www.robbiesamuels.com/favorite-things.

PART THREE: ENGAGE YOUR NETWORK

My Pandemic Reinvention

Before 2020, I'd spent over a decade building up my expertise and authority around networking and relationship-building with a focus on events and conferences.

On March 9, 2020, it became clear that my expertise and what I taught—eye contact, business cards, body language, and handshakes—were not going to be relevant for the foreseeable future.

I'd been paying attention to the news overseas earlier in the year, so I accepted the reality as it was happening. Still, I struggled with the question of how to show up and add value in a fast-changing world. Fortunately, I had a meeting with my peer mastermind group two days later. They gave me the nudge that I needed to take action.

The next day, I wrote and shared *9 Ways to Network in a Pandemic*[1] with my network. Later that night, I decided to try out one of the ideas. Looking at the list, it became obvious that I should host a virtual happy hour, since I love to convene people and I'd made it a habit to host networking dinners.

I had been active in Dorie Clark's private Recognized Expert Facebook group[2] for several years. I posted a note and immediately received several affirmative responses.

And that's how I ended up hosting a virtual happy hour on March 13, 2020[3]—the same day that the world paused. I wasn't trying to start a new business, I just wanted to show up and add immediate value.

Fast forward. That decision led to the creation of several new revenue streams and a thriving six-figure business. I'll share more on the details of that new business in a later chapter. For now, let's look at how my network made this reinvention possible.

- I was actively engaged in several Facebook groups, including sharing resources, encouraging other members, and scheduling lots of "get to know you" calls.
- I took the initiative in 2018 to create and facilitate a peer mastermind group. The specific people in the group changed over those years, but I had continuous access to a small group of committed entrepreneurs who know me and what I can do, as well as what holds me back.
- I had built a habit of offering value and making that a priority over making a profit. My philosophy of abundance leads me to believe that giving away knowledge makes my network stronger and leads to new possibilities.

Wake Up Your Network

I believe that you've already met 80% of the people you need to know to be successful.

Networking isn't all about meeting new people, but it's largely about deepening connections with people in your existing network.

When I first started working with Stacy, she was trying to figure out how her skills and experience could be translated into a profitable offer. She felt she needed to focus on being recognized as an expert before she would be able to test out her ideas with prospective clients. From my perspective, despite having considerable life experience, deep knowledge of her topic, and an extensive network built over a 30-year career—self-doubt was holding Stacy back.

Don't get me wrong. I too subscribe to the belief that being recognized as an expert makes it easier to attract clients. I've been following and implementing Dorie Clark's work on this topic for many years.[4] I just don't think it's necessary to wait until some magical moment in the future —when you finally feel "recognized" as an expert—to engage your network around your topic and see how you can add value in the form of a paid offer.

You may wonder how to determine what offer would be most appealing to your network while seeking out opportunities to write for high-profile publications, get quoted in industry news outlets, and create content that showcases your knowledge.

The best place to start is assessing your network so you know whom to contact and what you'd like to discuss with them. In the next section, I'll share how to conduct "research calls" so you can thoughtfully engage your network in ways that lead to a successful launch.

What happened to Stacy? She followed the steps in the Challenge below and began connecting regularly with her network. When the pandemic began, her niche was suddenly flooded with "experts" and she needed to find ways to differentiate herself—and quickly. Through research calls, Stacy discovered a new niche that was just emerging. It became clear that her background and experience were well suited for this new opportunity, which would allow her to differentiate herself in a now-overcrowded market. Stacy pursued this opportunity and based on the strength of past relationships; she won a multi-five-figure contract. That was just her first sale.

Assessing your network isn't just about identifying likely prospects. As you're working to take your business to the next level, you'll want to surround yourself with people who will guide you, hold you accountable, inspire you, and support you. If you're not intentional about who these people are, you may find yourself getting advice from people who don't have your best interest in mind or can't envision the world you're striving to create for yourself.

To be intentional and focused, create a list of people with whom you want to stay in touch over the next year. This is an ever-evolving list of people that you intentionally want to know better and with whom you'd like to have a deeper relationship over time. A small percentage will be people you have yet to meet, but who you believe can have a positive impact on your ability to meet your goals. But let's start with the 80% you've already met.

Your Challenge: Wake Up Your Network

Download "Wake Up Your Network" as a workbook and other book resources at www.robbiesamuels.com/toolkit.

Create a list of 50 or more people with whom you will intentionally engage over the next year. These will be a mix of former colleagues, old friends, former classmates—*all of whom would remember your name and you would welcome hearing from them out of the blue.*

This is *not* just a list of likely prospects, as I've found my clients often overlook likely referral partners and underestimate the power of referrals. If you put energy into waking up your network to what you do, you'll inevitably discover prospects and build a strong referral network.

1) Download a .csv file of your LinkedIn contacts.
If you're not familiar with how to do this, go to Google and search for "Export Connections from LinkedIn" to find the steps. Not using LinkedIn? Now's the time to join! But you

can also create a spreadsheet using your phone contacts, email address book, or Facebook friends.

2) Insert six columns at the front of the spreadsheet: Consider, Category, Connection, Influence, Interest, Total.

Without spending too much time on any one person, quickly scan through the list and put an 'x' in the **Consider** column for anyone you want to assess later.

Remember, the only criteria right now are whether they remember your name and if you would welcome hearing from them out of the blue.

Don't overthink this step and worry if you might end up with a list of 200+ people. That's a great problem to have. I'll show you how to sort and prioritize the group of people you select in the next step.

Consider	Category	Connection	Influence	Interest	Total	First Name
x	Referral Partner	3	3	2	8	Dorie
x	Likely Prospect	2	1	3	6	Tammy
x	Coffee Chat	3	1	1	5	Tracie
z		2	1	1	4	Jess

3) Assess the list and prioritize outreach based on their Connection, Influence, and Interest.

Once you have a list of at least 50 contacts marked with an 'x' in the **Consider** column, it's time to do a quick assessment. For each of the following, rank contacts a 1, 2, or 3 with three meaning "most" and one meaning "least." Don't enter half numbers, such as 2.5.

Rank Connection from 1-3: If you have a strong connection to this contact and know they would respond quickly to your message, enter a 3 in the **Connection** column. If it's been years since you last spoke and you're not sure they would respond at all, enter a 1 in the **Connection** column. Do they fall somewhere in between those extremes? Enter a 2 in the **Connection** column.

Rank Influence 1-3: If a contact has a large following and could direct their network to support your work, enter a 3 in the **Influence** column. If the contact largely keeps to themselves, does not have a position of authority, and has not cultivated a following, enter a 1 in the **Influence** column. Not sure their influence warrants a 3 but you're certain 1 would not be accurate? Enter a 2 in the **Influence** column.

Rank Interest 1-3: If you have an offer in mind, what level of interest do you suspect this contact would have? Do their social media posts lead you to believe they have a strong passion for this topic? Based on their job title, do you believe they have a strong need for your solution? Enter a 3 in the **Interest** column. If your gut tells you that they have no interest in this topic, enter a 1 in the **Interest** column. Not certain how interested they'd be? Enter a 2 in the **Interest** column.

4) Add up these numbers and enter the sum into the Total column.

Using Excel, Numbers, or Google Sheets, it's easy to automate tallying these numbers using a formula. Enter the formula =SUM(C2:E2) in cell F2. Then copy cell F2, highlight from F3 to F250, and paste the formula into these cells.

5) If the sum was 4 or 3 change the 'x' in the Consider column to a 'z.'

You have limited time, so best to not focus energy on a contact that does not rank very high in any of the three criteria.

Mark them with a 'z' to put them on pause in a way that allows you to review this group again at a later date to see if your answers have changed.

Sort the **Consider** column A-Z so those marked 'z' drop to the bottom of the list.

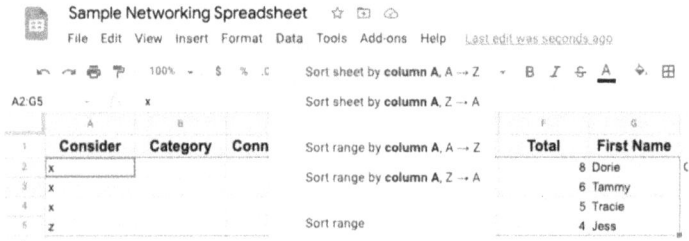

6) Assign the remaining contacts to a category.

Review the remaining contacts:

- If they have high Influence and high Interest, mark them as a **Referral Partner** in the **Category** column.

- If they have low Influence and high Interest, mark them as a **Prospect** in the **Category** column.
- Mark everyone else as **Coffee Chat** in the **Category** column.

Did you discover any strong prospects? I was sharing this process at a training session and one of the participants discovered that her mechanic was an ideal prospect. He happened to be the first person in her phone contacts. She had never thought to talk to him about her work.

7) Get excited because you're now ready to do "research calls."

You may not yet be sold on the need to schedule calls with likely prospects because you're certain you, as the expert, know exactly what they need.

Beware Expert Syndrome

While I was writing this book, I started dreaming up a new offer that got me really excited.

If I followed the course of action I took in my early years of being an entrepreneur, this is what I would have done next:

- Create the program out of the public eye with no input from likely prospects.
- Watch hours of YouTube videos to figure out how to best record video content.
- Pay for a learning management system (e.g., Thinkific or Teachable) and then spend hours figuring out how to set up a course with a payment option.
- Price the program by picking a number out of a hat.
- Hastily put together a sales page without any expert advice.

Then, after being disappointed by the lack of response, I would have felt like I'd spent way too much money and time to change course now.

Sound familiar?

I call this **expert syndrome,** because it's likely to happen most frequently to people who know a lot about their topic.

They are so certain that they have the perfect solution that they don't see any need to slow down and check in with likely prospects.

They don't build a runway for their idea to launch because no one knows about it until the day it launches.

Fortunately, I've learned from the error of my ways and now always do research and testing before I launch.

This is often through a series of one-on-one calls with likely prospects to better understand how *they* see the problem and what *they* are looking for in a solution.

I also weave in calls with fellow experts to get a better understanding of the current landscape and how I could add value with my skill and experience.

Whenever I explain my process, someone has a story to share about a failed launch that left them feeling like a failure.

One of my clients said, "No one ever talks about failed launches so I didn't have anyone with whom I could process this."

In hindsight, it makes sense that creating a program without input from likely prospects isn't our best option.

Why then is this such a familiar experience?

When you're an expert, it seems incredibly obvious to you what the problem is and how to solve that problem.

Your likely prospects, though, are not experts.

The way they see the problem is quite different and that's where we go wrong.

This isn't a new issue either, since Eugene Schwartz tackled this in his classic book *Breakthrough Advertising* back in 1966.[5]

I learned about a version of this concept first from Danny Iny, founder of Mirasee,[6] and then later another twist was added by Jason Van Orden, long-time host of *Internet Business Mastery* podcast and now the host of the *IMPACT* podcast.[7]

They are both well-respected business strategists.

Your likely prospects are at a different level of awareness than you.

They are symptom-aware—meaning they have small 'p' problems that they'd like to resolve but they have no sense that this is part of a bigger 'P' problem.

And that's why research calls are so helpful.

Through research calls, you'll learn the exact problem language used by likely prospects and you'll be able to shift your marketing to meet them where they are.

Let's say you have a rash on your arm that keeps reappearing.

You might be looking for some anti-itch cream to solve the itchiness you're experiencing.

You come to me with that solution in mind and I diagnose your rash as poison ivy.

Through a line of questioning, I determine poison ivy is all over your backyard and that's why you keep experiencing this.

My solution? I suggest that you call a guy I know who will bring a bulldozer over to raze your yard down to dirt so you're sure to get rid of all the poison ivy.

Is that a solution you're ready to buy when you come to me for anti-itch cream?

Probably not, as it feels incredibly disproportionate from what you were expecting me to suggest.

We need to help likely prospects move from symptom-aware to problem-aware, then they'll be more open to hearing about our solution.

This should be the focus of your marketing messages and research calls—helping your prospects realize their little 'p' problem is part of a much bigger 'P' problem.

The full journey is from **symptom-aware** to **problem-aware** to **solution-aware** to **you-aware** to **now-aware**. The first three levels of awareness I learned from Danny Iny. He also includes **unaware** (if someone is unaware then they definitely are *not* a likely prospect). The last two levels I learned from Jason Van Orden. Once someone is solution-aware are they aware that YOU can provide that solution? And are they aware of the cost of inaction if they delay taking action?

It's time to start moving likely prospects along these stages of awareness by conducting research calls.

Can I Skip Research Calls if I ...?

You may still not be convinced you should take time to meet individually with likely prospects. You're raring to get started with some type of new program. You want to develop a new revenue stream in your business and you want it to be a one-to-many program of some kind. You're not sure whether your clients would be best served by an in-person event, an online course, a virtual group coaching program, a mastermind, or some combination of these.

Consider this scenario. You heard my message that you shouldn't develop your new offer without input from likely clients, but you feel you have enough information from the *Finding Your Ideal Client* exercise to move forward quickly. It's true that may lead you to realize that you already have people coming to you for advice, support, or services, but you haven't thought to offer them the option to work with you in a group program.

You may have discovered that you have an **adjacent expertise** that you hadn't thought to monetize. Adjacent expertise is experience you've developed around a process that helps you achieve a business goal.

You decide to host a free online training course. You set up a landing page so you can collect email addresses as people register. You then spread the word to your network—

in particular, reaching out to anyone who has asked you for this advice in the last year.

You create a handout to give to everyone who signs up and you use this as a guide for what you'll present during the live video session. You plan for 30-45 minutes of content, so there's plenty of time for questions from anyone who attends live. Thirty-five people register, only six attend live, but you still get great engagement during the session.

After the session ends, you send the replay video and the handout to everyone who signed up. To determine if there's serious interest, you offer a 20-minute chat with anyone who has additional questions. You also offer an introductory coaching package at a price point that lets you know people are willing to pay you for the value you offer (e.g., $1,000 for four sessions).

What happens next? Often, it's crickets.

The six people who attended the free online training may feel they got what they needed because your program didn't move them from **symptom-aware** to **problem-aware**—so they're not seeking a more comprehensive solution. They also didn't pay for the information, so they haven't prioritized implementing the strategies you shared.

Of the twenty nine people who received the replay, only two watched it all the way through and that was while they were multi-tasking (washing dishes or answering emails). Most of this group didn't even open the email that shared the replay because they weren't looking for it and the email went to the promotions tab in Gmail.

You'd planned to move people from these shorter four-session coaching engagements to a longer three or even six-month coaching package, but after months of effort, only one person signs up for the four-session package.

After six months of half-heartedly trying to find an audience for your offer, you move it to the back burner because you're now excited about a new idea. You repeat this process and get the same results.

If by some chance you do line up clients from your efforts, they will all be one-on-one clients and your calendar will quickly be filled. But wouldn't it be better to create a one-to-many program that's easily filled by an audience craving your solution? Then you can better manage your schedule and your energy while having a greater impact and income.

Ready to try a different way?

Ask Before Building

"Target market research" sounds a lot more complicated than "talk to a few friends," but essentially that's what the next step entails. Actually, "listen to a few friends" would be a more accurate description.

Too often, when an entrepreneur has an opportunity for a research call with a likely prospect, they focus on pitching their idea and asking for feedback. This narrows the conversation to the pros and cons of that specific idea, which may not be the solution the likely prospect had in mind.

Instead of describing all the features of your latest and greatest program, tell them the topic on which you're focused and ask them to share the challenges they face. The key is to listen to the exact wording they use to describe these challenges.

This is their **problem language.** If you pay attention, you'll notice it's not how you would describe their problem. That's because you're solution-aware and they're symptom-aware. If your marketing is focused on the solution, your message won't resonate with your target audience.

Consider this:

The symptom is the patient has an annoying rash that keeps reappearing.

You know the cause is poison ivy, which is all over their backyard.

You also know the solution is to remove this plant from their backyard by any means necessary.

If you advertise bulldozers as the remedy for their itch, it will be a serious mismatch. Your prospects are not ready for this big solution because they're not yet aware of the big problem. Offer them anti-itch cream but use this as an opportunity to discuss the actual cause of their recurring rash and explain how it's likely to keep happening. Anti-itch cream won't stop the problem long-term. But understanding the cause of the problem may make them more open to choosing the solution that removes the problem.

What to Ask

You now understand that your goal is to listen and not pitch, but you may be wondering how to structure the conversation.

Reach out to likely prospects on your list via email. Let them know you're working on a new offer and would like their feedback before you get too far into the process. Mention specifically why you feel they would have valuable insights based on their experience or situation. Ask them to meet with you via Zoom for twenty to thirty minutes.

When they agree, coordinate a time to meet, and ask them to prepare by brainstorming three questions to ask you. This could be three scenarios, three problems, three challenges, etc.

Once the meeting starts and you've thanked the

prospect for their time, ask them to share their three questions. Instead of immediately giving away lots of free advice, take ten to fifteen minutes to explore why they chose these three questions.

- Are these the most urgent problems they're facing within this context?
- What's been the impact of these issues on their business? What about their personal life?
- What remedies have they tried? Why haven't they worked?
- What remedy has been most successful for them?
- What do they think is getting in their way?
- Now that they're talking about this, can they think of any other problems that might need to be addressed first?

Through this line of questioning, they will begin to see how these little "p" problems fit together and are causing a bigger "P" problem in their business or life. This is moving them from symptom-aware to problem-aware.

Wrap up the call by sharing what you see as their big "P" problem and offering high-level next steps to consider. Invite them to reach out if they have any questions as they implement your suggestions.

Make it clear that your feedback is based on a limited understanding of their business. When you work with your clients, you don't diagnose and create a treatment plan without a much deeper dive into the root cause of the problem. Let them know you'll circle back with an update as you progress with creating your new offer and thank them profusely for their time and insights.

The Free Advice Pitfall

If you're like most entrepreneurs, the scenario I just described won't feel very familiar. Here's what I suspect usually happens when someone asks to "pick your brain" or you reach out asking for their feedback on an offer.

You spend an hour giving away free advice—solid and actionable free advice. You feel pretty good about yourself at the end of the meeting because you like being helpful and you feel you've shared your expertise. You probably mention five, maybe even ten, tactics they could try based on your very limited understanding of their problem.

Have you noticed that people who get an hour of free advice very, very rarely sign up to work with you? That's a bit irksome, but you keep doing this because these great ideas pour into your head as you're speaking with them. You can't stop yourself from sharing.

Let's look at this from the perspective of the likely prospect. They also feel great about how the call went and they take copious notes. They're excited to try some of your suggestions. They may feel a bit overwhelmed now because they're starting to realize that what they thought was a small "p" problem is actually a big "P" problem. They're not sure where to start with the five to ten tactics you shared and they begin to doubt their ability to implement these ideas.

They write down notes on their to-do list and a few weeks later they're not able to remember the specifics. Maybe they try one tactic and run into a snag right away. Either way, more than a month later, the copious notes they took are buried under a pile of papers and they haven't made any notable progress based on your free advice.

When they come across you online or see you at an event, they feel bad for not taking action, since you were so generous with your expertise. Rather than reach out to you for more advice, they start to avoid you while promising themselves they'll make time to implement your ideas.

Sound familiar?

People rarely act on free advice, especially a list of hastily scribbled tactics that are not part of a strategic plan. I know it's difficult, but you'll need to resist sharing lots and lots of great advice and focus instead on helping them become more aware of their big "P" problem. Once they're more aware, they'll become more open to hearing about possible solutions. The benefits of having you as their coach or guide will become readily apparent and they'll be asking for your advice on the next steps.

Setting Up for Success

The second most common pitfall many entrepreneurs experience is not taking steps to record, transcribe, and analyze all the juicy "problem language" shared during these calls. Taking notes will not suffice, because you need to capture the exact words used to describe challenges. Taking notes will be helpful for a quick reference to remind yourself about the call, but won't be as beneficial when writing marketing copy.

Fortunately, technology makes recording a lot easier than when we had to carry around cumbersome tape recorders. Zoom is ideal for research calls, as it is simple to record and much easier to gauge people's responses when you can see their body language. By default, Zoom recordings are saved in the Documents folder on your computer.

Zoom has the ability to transcribe Zoom Meetings at no additional cost. Go to **Settings** on www.zoom.us, then click on **In Meetings** (**Advanced**), to enable closed captioning.

Check the box for *Allow live transcription service to transcribe meeting automatically.* The transcription is produced by artificial intelligence (AI), so you may need to review the recording to create a more accurate transcript.[8]

Before you dive into scheduling and recording these calls, determine how you'll analyze all of the data you'll collect. If you don't have this in place, you'll quickly become overwhelmed by the volume of data you're gathering. To avoid this, schedule time after each call to review the transcript, highlight problem language, and copy that text onto a spreadsheet.

I'll go into greater detail on how to analyze the problem language at the end of the *Pay Attention to Patterns* section. For now, it's important to build time into your schedule to do this on an ongoing basis. Don't wait until you've recorded ten or more conversations before you start this part of the process!

Ready for Research Calls?

You are now on the precipice of what once felt like an impossible quest.

- You know to ask before you build a new offer.
- You now have a list of likely prospects.
- You know the importance of listening instead of pitching.
- You have a sense of what to ask during these conversations.
- You know not to spend the entire time giving away free advice.
- You're prepared to record and transcribe via Zoom.

- You've set aside time to analyze the data you're collecting.

I'm certain you still have questions. You may be feeling a bit uncertain about how well this will go. That's why I recommend you begin by scheduling a few virtual "coffee" chats. This is a low-key way to practice talking about your topic. If you have not yet done so, create a system for tracking your outreach efforts. You can easily schedule meetings using a calendar link, such as OnceHub or Calendly.

Setting up a calendar link is going to be a game-changer. Years ago, before I had the ability to easily schedule meetings, I found the back-and-forth emails necessary to schedule a meeting to be very tedious. Sometimes it was easier to decline a coffee chat invitation than take the time to schedule it when I was busy.

I'm most familiar with OnceHub, formerly known as ScheduleOnce, as that's what I use. On the book resource page, I'm including steps for setting up your account so you have the ability to block out specific times on your calendar for research calls, approve/decline meeting requests, and have a 15-minute buffer between calls. I've included other tips to make scheduling a breeze. Most of these features are available in other software options, too.

Watch a video with these tips and find other book resources at www.robbiesamuels.com/toolkit.

Getting Started with Research Calls

Look at your **Wake Up Your Network** list and identify fifteen to twenty likely prospects you'd like to contact for research calls. Start with people with whom you have a strong connection and who have a strong interest in your topic.

Identify three to five fellow experts who can give you a sense of this market and share the challenges their clients often face. (Remember: You're aiming to fill a gap in the market, not duplicate services, unless you have a strong differentiator.)

Send an email to likely prospects. Keep it friendly and don't write a novel. Let them know you're working on a new offer. Before you get too far into the process, you'd like to hear their take on their challenges, since they have personal experience in this area. Ask if they'd be willing to meet for thirty minutes. Don't include your calendar link at this point. Share it after they agree to meet.

Send a similar email to fellow experts. Ask if they'd be willing to meet to share their experience with the demographic on which you're focusing. Let them know you want a better sense of what's already being offered so you can make referrals, since not everyone will be a good fit for you.

Be sure to track all initial and follow-up emails on the spreadsheet. Adding additional columns for **Initial Email, Follow-up 1,** and **Follow-up 2** will help you keep things organized. Send the first follow-up message four to seven days later, and the second follow-up message three to five days after that. Enter the date each message was sent in the appropriate column. Add a column for **Meeting** to track when the meeting is scheduled.

Once a likely prospect accepts your invitation, send them your calendar link. Ask them to come to the meeting with three questions/problems/scenarios to discuss. You'll spend fifteen minutes discussing why they chose these. You'll want to draw out how urgent these issues are, what remedies they've already tried, what solutions they think they need, etc. Your goal is to move them from symptom-aware to problem-aware.

During the second half of the call, offer your insight into the problem (which is very likely a bigger picture than what they had just said). Share possible ways to move forward, making it clear that you can't possibly be prescribing the exact solution, since you've only been discussing this for a few minutes. Resist giving away an hour of free advice. Encourage them to reach out to you as they test out these ideas, as they will likely encounter obstacles or have additional questions.

Thank them for taking the time to share their insights. Let them know that you may be back in touch to ask a few more questions once you've had time to digest these calls. If their answers confirm this is your ideal client, your goal is to build a win-win relationship with them, not have a one-time conversation.

Your Challenge: Schedule fifteen to twenty research calls

Identify fifteen to twenty likely prospects and three to five fellow experts from your **Wake Up Your Network** list.

Draft an email inviting them to meet with you. Reread your email and make it shorter. Don't go into great detail.

Send an email to three to five likely prospects and one fellow expert. Personalize the opening line of each email so it feels more like a conversation between friends than from a bot.

Note on your calendar when you'll send follow-up messages if they don't respond.

In three or four days, send another email to five additional likely prospects and one more fellow expert. Repeat every few days until you've sent a message to everyone you've identified.

Aim to schedule all meetings within three to six weeks. Don't let this drift on for months!

Don't forget to hit record and enable live transcription. Upload the recording and transcript to Google Drive or Dropbox so you have a backup copy—just in case your computer stops working properly.

Within twenty-four hours, review the transcript and highlight the problem language. Follow the steps in the next section to analyze this data.

Pay Attention to Patterns

Did you remember to hit record and enable live transcription? Excellent. That means you have hours and hours of video, plus pages and pages of transcripts. It's tempting to skip analyzing this data. Every coaching client I've helped through this process has initially resisted this step. And every coaching client who did follow through discovered something that helped them move their idea to the next stage: piloting the concept.

You may feel you heard something during these calls that confirms your big idea. That's exciting! It means you're on the right track and now need to get clarity on how to best market your offer to attract your target audience. That clarity will be found in this data.

Many entrepreneurs with whom I've worked have told me they thought the way to launch an offer was all about creating a sales page and then driving traffic towards that site. They hired consultants to help them create Facebook ads, but the sales page didn't convert. It's an understatement to say they were disappointed with the results of their efforts. That's because they hadn't clarified what little "p" problems their likely prospects wanted to resolve and what specific outcome would be most enticing.

You might have learned through these calls that what you initially thought was a brilliant idea for a new offer isn't aligned with the little "p" problems that were most deeply felt. It may not feel like it, but that's actually good news. Learning that now will save you months or even years of effort, not to mention likely a lot of money on consultants, marketing, and software.

Instead, take a deeper look at what people said during these calls and how they said it. The goal is to find patterns and ultimately to figure out what offer would resonate most strongly with an urgent need you heard expressed during these calls.

Urgent is key. If a small "p" problem is chronic, there's a good chance the likely prospect isn't looking for a solution. In some ways, they've learned to live with this chronic issue and might be resistant to trying new ideas after so many other efforts didn't work out. It's not chronic if this is a long-term problem they've been struggling to overcome and they're still looking for answers.

How do you know whether the problem is long-term or chronic? How did the prospect sound as they shared a laundry list of solutions they tried? Exasperated or resigned? Are they asking for new ideas or telling you, "It is, what it is?"

If they have an acute small "p" problem, their need to find a solution will be more urgent. They'll be more open to learning about new options. If the issue with which they're dealing is a recent development, they may now be actively seeking a solution. They may be trying random remedies without anyone to guide them or provide strategy. Maybe initially they thought they could figure this issue out on their own and it's now beginning to dawn on them that they need help.

You may be wondering how you can tell whether someone is talking about an issue/challenge/problem that's urgent. Some of this is in the way they speak, which is why you'll want to copy their problem language into a spreadsheet and note the urgency of the statement while the conversation is still fresh in your mind. Another factor is how long they speak about that specific issue.

For example, if your topic is productivity and you ask people whether or not they feel like they get enough sleep, you may hear people say, "I don't get enough sleep." If that phrase or ones like it keep coming up in conversations, you may think that developing a course around how to get more sleep to help with productivity would be a great idea.

But "I don't get enough sleep" is not on its own an urgent problem statement. If you build a course around a common but not deeply felt problem, it will be difficult to find an audience willing to pay for the course. People pay to fix problems that they feel are urgent.

Within twenty-four hours after each research call, review the transcript and highlight the problem language. Use one color to highlight short problem statements and another to highlight long ones. This way your brain won't immediately lock onto the commonly held but not deeply felt language which keeps popping up over and over but isn't what people will pay for.

In response to your question around sleep, you may have heard variations, such as:

"I definitely don't get enough sleep. I try to have a bedtime routine and to go to sleep at the same time each night, but I feel like I always have more work to finish.

Then, I end up going to sleep past midnight knowing I'll be woken up by my kids at 6 am. I spring into action in the morning, but I'm dragging by 10 am. Coffee is what keeps me going. I'm jittery, though, by midday, and let's just say my mood is not great. I try to keep it together at work, but I have zero patience left by the time I get home. It's causing a strain on my relationship with my family. And yet, I find myself doing it again each night. If only I could feel good about my to-do list I might be able to stop being so grouchy and exhausted."

If you speak with twenty people and you hear something similar at least four times, that's worth further investigation. When you discover something causing a strain on relationships and/or impacting work, that issue has urgency.

Now you can create a course around productivity and market it towards people who have this problem. This is how to differentiate yourself in a crowded market. People who don't feel productive because they have trouble getting enough sleep will be drawn to this course. Prospects will identify with the language used in the promotional materials and the course description.

Notice how the word "exhausted" was repeated in the long problem statement? Check to see if there are words used consistently by other likely prospects. If so, use them in your marketing materials. Without doing these research calls, you might have instead used the word "fatigued," even though you now realize that not a single person used that word.

That's because "fatigued" is a word used by experts like yourself and "exhausted" is the word people use to describe themselves. If your course description used the word "fatigue," it would not resonate as strongly with likely prospects.

You know you're on the right track when someone reads your course description or other marketing material and thinks, "It's as if she's reading my mind!" I get this response quite often from my email subscribers.

Here's a comment I received recently:

"Yes! Letting go is so hard and so important. Many of your posts resonate perfectly. Are you reading my journal? ;)"

Your Challenge: Analyze the Problem Language

Download "Analyze the Problem Language" as a workbook and other book resources at www.robbiesamuels.com/toolkit.

As I mentioned earlier, don't fall into the trap of believing you can skip this step. It isn't rocket science but it does require grit to see it through. The benefits are numerous, including being able to clearly articulate the problem as experienced by the prospect, building trust with prospects and referral partners, and identifying participants for your pilot program.

Follow the suggested timeline after each research call so you don't end up with a backlog of a dozen transcripts to analyze. If you stay on top of this, you won't need to watch the videos after each session. And you may realize you need to tweak your script to ensure you gather the right information to help you.

Set up the spreadsheet: Before starting research calls, set up a spreadsheet to capture the problem language. Add these titles to the first six columns: **Name, Problem Statement, Urgency, Category 1, Category 2, Category 3.**

Highlight problem language: Within twenty-four hours of each research call, read through the transcript and highlight the problem language. Highlighting can be done electronically in a Google or Word doc, or you may want to print the transcript. Use one highlighter color for short statements and another for long statements. This will help you avoid latching onto a common problem that isn't deeply felt and therefore won't be a solution for which prospects will pay. You may need to refer to the video recording to clarify the text since the transcription is computer-generated.

Add problem language to the spreadsheet: Within forty-eight hours of each research call, copy the exact problem language into the spreadsheet. Enter a new row for each additional problem statement and always include the person's name so you can easily sort the spreadsheet later (i.e., the first person has ten rows with their name and problem statement, the next person has seven, etc.).

Note the urgency: After entering each problem statement, immediately note the urgency by entering a value from 1-10 (with 10 being most urgent) in the **Urgency** column. How will you know the urgency? It's a combination of how long they spoke about this issue and how they said it. That's why it's important to note urgency within forty-eight hours while the conversation is still fresh in your mind.

Categorize the problem statements: Once you've entered at least twelve problem language statements, it's time to start categorizing. Your aim is to discover common themes. Make the categories broad. Before you add a new category, double-check that an existing one won't suffice. For example, one person may say they don't feel like they belong, so you write down "*Belonging*" for the category. Someone else says "I don't feel included," and a third person says "I have trouble fitting in." Those should all go into the same category.

Download "Analyze the Problem Language" as a workbook and other book resources at www.robbiesamuels.com/toolkit.

What's Your Promise?

Once you've identified key themes, it's time to narrow them down to a specific problem on which you will focus. You're looking for a problem that has been experienced and considered urgent by at least three of the people to whom you spoke. Remember not to get hooked on a commonly felt but not urgent problem or you'll end up developing a solution that no one is looking to buy.

Before reaching out again to a select number of people who you feel might be ideal clients, take time to first develop your **minimally viable outcome,** or a promise. This is the outcome for which your ideal client is looking—something that would help them realize they are on the right track, even if it's not the full answer to what they now realize is a big "P" problem.

For example:

"After participating in this 6-week pilot, you will be able to…"

"After participating in this 6-week pilot, you will feel…"

"After participating in this 6-week pilot, you will know…"

You may have a six-month (or longer) program in mind, but start with a pilot program that is four to six weeks long. Obviously, the outcome from participating in a much longer program will be different than what's possible in just a few weeks.

I know it's tempting, but don't cram six months of content into six weeks! Consider the minimal information you need to convey for a participant to begin to see results.

This may often be the first one or two sections of a longer program. What would a participant be able to do after going through the first two sections of your full program?

This is different from a guarantee. A **guarantee** ensures a refund or extended support if they don't reach a specific, measurable milestone. A **promise** tells a prospective client what outcome they should expect *if they do the work*. It's the minimum viable outcome that every participant who takes action should experience. It isn't the outlier 10x result.

I run the Wake Up Your Network Program,[9] which consists of ten monthly mastermind sessions and two one-on-one calls. Here is that program's promise:

You will stop struggling to find an audience for your offers because you'll co-create an offer they can't resist. You'll be adept at implementing a repeatable process that helps you discover likely prospects from within your existing network who already know, like, and trust you.

Notice that I don't guarantee a specific revenue. That's because I have no control over how viable a participant's idea may be. What I *can* do is support them through a process that helps them quickly determine whether or not the idea is worth pursuing or learning if it needs to be adjusted or even scrapped. If their original idea turns out to be a dud, they will have discovered new problems from their likely prospects and can shift their focus to this more viable idea.

Now it's your turn. What is the promise for your pilot program? Remember, this isn't what a participant will achieve through your full program, just what they will gain from the sections in your initial trial program.

As you're considering the content and flow of your pilot, plan to have six to eight participants meet four, five, or six weeks in a row for a 90-minute or two-hour session. For reasons I'll explain later, I recommend a minimum of four participants and a max of twelve.

Test Your Assumptions

Now that you have an idea of your promise, a general sense of the structure of your session, and an outline of the content you'd cover in each session—it's time to test your assumptions.

Reach out to people with whom you've already spoken who would likely be seeking the outcome described in your promise. In your email, share that you've been working on developing a new program and that something they said keeps coming to mind. Be specific! Ask if they'd be willing to meet for another thirty minutes to share feedback on what you've developed so far. Thank them again for meeting with you the first time, because their insights were so helpful. Keep the message brief. Don't include either your promise or the program details in the email (i.e., don't mention the number of weeks or length of each session).

Start the meeting by thanking them again and repeating the problem language text you quoted in the email. Remind them you're developing a new program and it's important to you not to create this in a vacuum without input from your network.

Tell them that once you've confirmed that you're going in the right direction, you will develop a four to six week pilot program. If the pilot is successful, you'll develop this into a much longer program. You'd like their feedback on the promise statement for the pilot program—the outcome participants would expect to achieve.

Then, read your promise statement and be quiet. Their

response will tell you whether you've nailed it or if the statement needs work.

If their response is less enthusiastic, listen carefully. Don't become defensive or try to persuade them. They're sharing valuable information that may help you tweak this promise statement or lead to an idea for an entirely new offer. If this happens, thank them for their time and let them know you'll be considering their feedback.

If they say, "Have you been reading my journal?" or "You're in my head!" then congratulations! You're ready to move to the next step: making the ask.

Your Challenge: Testing Your Promise

- Review your problem language spreadsheet and identify six to twelve people who would likely be seeking this outcome.
- Draft emails inviting them to meet with you. Personalize each by quoting a specific problem that was shared.
- Don't share the program promise or details in your message, as your goal is to get a meeting, not provide feedback via email.
- Note on your calendar when you'll send follow-up messages if they don't respond.
- Aim to schedule all meetings within three to six weeks. Don't let this drift on for months.
- Don't forget to hit **record** and enable live transcription. Upload the recording and transcript to Google Drive or Dropbox so there's a backup copy—just in case your computer stops working properly.

Making the Ask

Before becoming a professional speaker and business growth strategist, I was the Senior Manager of Events and Donor Engagement at a regional LGBTQ nonprofit law firm with a national impact. I worked there for nearly ten years and that's where I honed my skills around asking. For many years, I offered a training session called *Fundraising: Getting Past the Fear of Asking*, based on my experience at this organization.

My mindset first began to shift from angst to awesome at a three-day retreat where participants were put into groups of six and told to develop a million-dollar pitch. That's right. We were all nervous about asking for money, and now we were put into a competition where we had to get on stage in front of the entire group to role-play asking for a million dollars.

To get started, the six of us were given a specific line to use. One by one, we took our turn saying this. Nearly every person, including me, had trouble saying these exact words:

"We're here to ask you to partner with us at the million-dollar level. Will you do that?"

Try it yourself. Did you deviate from this in some way? The most common change was switching the "Will you" to "Can you." I wasn't an English major, but that's an entirely different question. Hearing a "Yes" in response to a "Can you" question just confirms your suspicion that they *can* take a certain action, not that they *will* take it.

Did you notice your voice go up a bit at the end of the sentence? When we're nervous, this is more likely to happen and it makes us seem uncertain. Try reading this as a statement instead of a question:

"We're here to ask you to partner with us at the million-dollar level. Will you do that."

Another common mistake is to keep talking after making the ask—filling the air with more words until you've thoroughly confused and distracted the prospect. After you make your ask, be quiet. Have a glass of water nearby and take a small sip as you patiently wait to hear your prospect's response. Practice doing this until you can say your "ask" line calmly and then stay quiet.

OK. Now you're ready to offer an invitation to join the pilot.

If someone has been enthusiastic about your pilot program promise, then it's time to ask if they'd like to hear more about the pilot content and flow. If they agree, share a high-level outline—the number of sessions and a general idea of what content will be covered—then ask their thoughts.

If the call is going well and you feel they'd be a good fit in your pilot, invite them to join.

"I was thinking about our earlier conversation as I developed the pilot program outcome and outline. After our discussion today, it sounds like you would get great benefit from participating and I know you'll continue to share thoughtful feedback. Would you like to join the pilot?"

This is where they'll likely ask about the fee. Plan for this moment ahead of time by thinking through your pricing. The pilot program fee should be a fraction of what you'd charge for the full program. For example, you might charge $497 for a four-session pilot vs. $1497 for a full three-month program or $997 for five sessions vs. $4,997 for a six-month program. Don't let talk of pricing distract you from moving forward with research calls. Pricing is a topic that benefits from the support of a coaching or mastermind program.

Your goal is to have six to eight participants in your pilot program. I suggest a minimum of four because there's always a chance someone will miss a session. With fewer participants than four, it no longer feels like a group experience. Twelve participants is the most I would recommend, because more than that makes it difficult to have a full group discussion.

PART FOUR: TAKING THE LEAP

In the past, it was common practice to host pilot programs in person. However, it became clear during the pandemic that online programs can be extremely effective. As a plus, online programs allow you to draw participants from all over the world. With that in mind, as a virtual event design consultant and executive Zoom producer, I'm going to share tips for how to leverage digital tools (such as Zoom) to host your pilot program.

Survey, Survey, Survey

Congrats! You now have between four and twelve participants signed up for your pilot program. They've paid and received the Zoom link. You shared a general outline when you invited them to participate. Now it's time to further hone that outline based on the needs of this particular group of participants. These individuals have agreed to support you in creating a value-packed program. They were drawn in because of the co-creation approach you demonstrated during the research calls. Because they're open to co-creation, you can use this to personalize the pilot for participants. This is a selling point you should be sure to mention in your second research call! Keep asking for their feedback. Don't wing it.

Before the pilot program begins, survey your participants to better understand what challenges they face and identify questions they have about your overall topic. You can use Momentive (formerly SurveyMonkey) or a Google Form to ask a combination of open-ended questions and questions that ask for a response on a scale of 1-10. The latter is useful for gauging the comfort or experience of a participant with a particular subject. Use that information to finalize the topics you'll address in each weekly session.

Prior to each ninety-minute to two-hour session, send another survey asking participants what questions they have regarding that specific topic and assessing their comfort level with that content. This will help you further refine your content for the week.

Please don't plan ninety minutes of content for a ninety-minute session! Be sure to leave at least thirty minutes for questions and discussion. Focus on how to make the content engaging, rather than lecture-style, by incorporating Zoom polls, questions participants answer in chat, and breakout rooms for small group discussions.

After each session, send a brief evaluation survey asking for feedback about the value of the content and structure of the session. This allows you to experiment with a few different formats during the pilot and learn which is most beneficial for your members.

Invite all pilot participants to meet with you one-on-one for thirty minutes at the end of the program. This will be an opportunity to hear whether you met the promise you made about the outcome they would experience in this pilot. If it went well, invite them to record a video testimonial (if they're not camera-ready, get a transcript of their testimonial). Then let them know you plan to use all the feedback you gathered to iterate and expand this into a more comprehensive program. When that's available, you'll offer them an early bird option which will allow them to apply the amount they paid for the pilot towards the full program cost.

What's Next?

What you offer next will depend on the feedback you receive from pilot participants. I recommend that my coaching clients run a weekly pilot program with four to six sessions, and that their next iteration should be sessions held every two weeks. The number of sessions may or may not change, but adding an extra week between sessions creates the opportunity to assign pre-work or homework. This makes the program more experiential and allows participants to integrate the material into their lives.

Continue to make tweaks to the program content and structure as you receive feedback from the first few cohorts. This ongoing co-creation will help you develop a great resource to attract your ideal clients. Pay attention to the words used by participants to describe their experience working with you and weave these into your promotional materials together with participant testimonials.

Not all changes will produce the desired outcome. Set specific goals for each twelve-week sprint to be sure you're on track. If you run into a roadblock, identify what's in your way and reroute your way to success.

Following these methods could lead to charging 10x the pilot fee in a year or two for a program that includes live sessions with you (e.g., a group coaching program or mastermind,) or developing a course that includes limited live access to you (e.g., Q&A sessions).

Continue to enthusiastically create resources for your growing community of followers, because this is a topic about which you're passionate and you love seeing the impact you're having on their lives.

Slipping When You're Close to the Top

Have you seen the viral video of a bear cub climbing up a snow-covered mountainside? The cub's mama had gotten to the top quickly, but the cub kept slipping. Sometimes the cub slips way, way, way down the side of the mountain. Each time, the cub gets right back to climbing. Several times the cub was within a couple of feet of the ledge where the mama bear was standing before slipping down again. This went on for over ten minutes. It was mesmerizing. The sheer determination. The commitment to succeed. This did end well. The cub reached the top and went on its merry way with the mama bear.[1]

Have you ever been within a few feet of success, slipped for the umpteenth time, and decided to give up? This is all too common for entrepreneurs—especially when you're just getting started with a new product. We get close to success. But then we're not determined. We're not definite in our commitment. And we let our dreams slip from our grasp when we're so close to success. I get it. You're trying something new. This pilot program is a new idea and it's your own invention. It's your name on the line.

Keep Striving to the Next Level

Once you've launched a pilot program and then hosted your full program a couple of times, it's easy to think you can take your foot off the gas and coast a while. You've worked hard to get to this point and you may be happy to finally be making some decent money.

This is *not* the time to slow down. You're just getting started. Stretching yourself is the next step. Doing so will provide much more value and probably increase both your influence and your income.

Once you've established your credibility and started to attract clients willing to pay high fees for the value you can offer them, it's time to reassess your goals around this product and for your business as a whole.

When you were first setting your goals, you couldn't possibly think as big as you can now—because you hadn't yet proven that your idea would work. Now that you're attracting people to this offer, you need to set bigger goals.

What that looks like will be different for everyone. This is a great moment to join a mastermind group to get continuous feedback as you strive for a bigger goal and don't want to limit yourself. This is a moment where, once again, you really need a mindset shift.

You need to believe in what value you're offering and that you have even more value to add. This may entail extending the program from ninety days to six months to one year. It may be adding an in-person retreat at the beginning, middle, and/or end of the program. It may be tapping your network and inviting guest experts to present to your community.

As you expand your offer, keep listening to your ideal clients and confirm you're developing a program that will continue to be attractive to them. The lure of "shiny objects" is always a danger to a well-crafted program. If you get super jazzed about creating a Facebook group, podcast, mastermind, etc., but your ideal clients aren't on Facebook, don't listen to podcasts, or need technical training more than mastermind support —it just won't work.

That's why it's important that you try different options without being attached to the outcome. Keep the spirit of testing and iterating. Know that doing so creates more possibilities for you and your business.

Don't Rush To Evergreen

Another extreme I've seen is a rush to turn a pilot program into a high-priced evergreen program—one that is not time-sensitive and can be repeated as is for a long period of time and keep attracting customers. We've all been sold on the idea of passive income. *There is no such thing.* The people who are making money through passive income streams are also still working: They're just working smarter. They're testing and iterating. They know you can't create a piece of content once, immediately make it evergreen, and expect to make money. It just doesn't happen. Expectations around online courses are changing. Savvy customers know that they can access online content for very little to no money. They then expect a more personal touch if they invest in a more expensive course.

No matter how polished your videos, they're not sufficient on their own to attract higher-paying clients. You need to offer more value than free and low-cost courses. There should be human interaction with you and your members as well.

To make decent money from a lower cost evergreen

program you would need a very, very large audience. That's not reality for my clients and readers of this book. Selling a low-priced course to a company is one option, as they will find participants. Another option would be creating a course for LinkedIn Learning and eventually earning royalties. Two people who have done this really well this are Denise Jacobs, a speaker, author, and creativity evangelist,[2] and Dorie Clark, whom I've mentioned throughout this book. They have six and twenty-three courses respectively.[3] [4]

Rather than racing to turn your content evergreen, keep iterating until you've created a process for attracting ideal clients and delivering value. When you've done that consistently, strengthen your lead generation through joint venture partnerships or Facebook ads.

You may discover that a portion of your program could be offered asynchronously via videos, written material, or audio. That may even become an introductory offer that is evergreen and attracts people to your signature offer by moving them from symptom-aware to problem-aware to solution-aware.

In addition to developing this offer, work on being recognized as an expert, thought leader, or authority by writing for high-profile publications and seeking out clients who would add credibility to your portfolio. It's much easier to charge higher fees once your credibility and expertise are readily apparent to prospective clients.

Connect with Influencers and Up Level Your Network

As you stretch your goals for your new product, you'll also want to stretch your goals for building and sustaining your professional network as well. It's time to connect with bigger influencers in your space.

Reach out and get to know people who operate at a higher level. These are individuals attracting higher-paying clients and taking steps in their business that you don't yet feel ready to try.

You may have heard the phrase, "You're the average of the five people with whom you spend the most time." This quote is most often attributed to motivational speaker Jim Rohn.[5] Yes, you're influenced by these five people, but it doesn't stop there. You are influenced by your network well beyond these five people.

In his book *Friend of a Friend...: Understanding the Hidden Networks That Can Transform Your Life and Your Career*, David Burkus shared how studies on the breadth of social influence have been conducted by Nicholas Christakis and James Fowler. They found that you're influenced by your friends, their friends, and their friends of friends.[6]

Re-examine the ocean in which you're swimming. Make a plan to shift your network over the next year so that you're surrounded by high achievers and their high achieving friends and friends of friends.[7]

My Philosophy of Abundance

Consider your mindset when it comes to making new connections. If you approach these new contacts in a way that feels like begging or stalking, it's not going to make a good impression.

I operate with a theory I call the philosophy of abundance. This influences how I show up in the world, including how I interact with major influencers in my field.

Years ago, back when I had a BlackBerry in the early 2000s, I'd agree to meet with people for coffee and answer questions they had about their career or business. I'd schedule two to four meetings a month an hour before I started working at a coffee shop one block from my office.

I would show up with my BlackBerry and my brain. They would show up with questions.

My mother got wind of this after I'd been doing these meetings for about two years and said, "Don't give it all away. You need to be paid for this."

I knew that what I was doing went beyond a monetary value and was building rapport, trust, and deeper connections within my network that would benefit me in ways I could not yet imagine.

I explained it to my mother this way:

I told her I saw this as similar to giving rides to the airport. You only give rides to the airport if you have a relationship with someone and you have the resources they need: time and a car. The person accepting the ride recognizes this as a favor and appreciates it.

Over time, you become known as someone who regularly gives rides to the airport. Then, one day *you* need a ride. You're going to get one—and quite possibly it may not be from someone who accepted a ride from you. It'll be someone who sees you as the kind of person who gives rides to the airport.

People want to support people who are givers.

Building your network with high-achieving people is easier once you start to look for ways to "give rides to the airport." Look for small ways you can be offering support and sharing your expertise.

As Bob Burg, co-author of *The Go-Giver,* says, being a go-giver is "understanding that shifting one's focus from getting to giving, in this case constantly and consistently providing value to others, is not only a nice way to live life but a very financially profitable way as well."[8]

Become known as a giver and you'll attract other givers.

This philosophy of abundance is a practice of asking yourself, "How do I show up and add value?" Always think about how to be generous as you're invited onto bigger stages. Keep showing up and keep offering.

PART FIVE: GETTING SUPPORT

You can't get where you want to go with your business on your own. You need support. What that support looks like will change and morph over time. It can sometimes be confusing to sort out what help would be most beneficial at the moment.

I'm going to guide you through a variety of support options for business owners. Each has pros and cons. Some are free and others cost quite a bit, but all require you to put your own time and energy into the relationship to really make a significant difference in your business.

Accountability Partner

If you've ever asked a friend to go to the gym with you, you've already experienced the power of an accountability partner. You both had the goal of getting in great shape. Even on those days you didn't feel like getting to the gym, you felt you had to follow through on your commitment because you knew your friend was there waiting for you.

What does that look like in the world of business? Fairly similar, actually. Accountability partners are great for project-based goals with clear deadlines or clear outcomes. They're not forever. Ideally, your accountability partner is working on a project that has a similar timeframe as yours, so they share the intensity of staying focused and avoiding distractions. They want to be held accountable for their work, while keeping you on track with your project.

Weekly check-ins of thirty to sixty minutes provide the structure and support you both need to check in about your progress, share any challenges you've faced in the last week, and give each other the pep talk you need to keep going when you're in the messy middle and don't yet see an end in sight.

You may balk at the idea of using some of your limited time each week doing these check-ins. It's not a question of time, though, if it gets you the clarity you need to stay engaged with your project and committed to seeing results. If you're feeling stuck or not making as much progress as you'd hoped, your accountability partner will be there to cheer you on and help you stay the course.

The only con of having an accountability partner is when they're not committed to doing their own project. If you're having trouble scheduling check-in calls or they slack off and disappear—that's problematic. That's why it's important to carefully choose someone who will stick with you. It's helpful to let them know up front that this is project-based and that you will be setting an end date.

The Power of a Coach

What's the difference between an accountability partner and a coach? A business coach is knowledgeable about the challenges you face and already lives the path you're trying to walk. Therefore, they can help you steer clear of major pitfalls by asking the right questions and helping you find your way to your goals.

It's great if your accountability partner can do that, but it's more likely they'll ask, "Did you do what you said you were going to accomplish last week?" If you reply that something got in your way, they'll ask, "What are the ways to get around that? What do you plan to do next week?" That's accountability, not coaching.

A coach, on the other hand, would ask, "What's at the root of why you're not getting this done? What's holding you back? What do you need to learn? Whom do you need to know for this to be more successful?" A coach will be more probing while keeping you accountable.

You will likely not speak with a coach as frequently as with an accountability partner. You might meet with a coach every two weeks or once a month. In between, the coach will assign homework to help you focus your energy on the right tasks to get you to your goals more quickly. An accountability partner is quite beneficial when you're working with a coach, as they'll help you stay on task in between your coaching sessions.

Why wouldn't you meet with a coach weekly instead of with an accountability partner? One main difference between these two forms of support is one is free and the other might cost several hundred dollars to a thousand dollars plus an hour.

Having a coach is an investment in yourself. Going back to the gym analogy, it would be like going to the gym with a professional trainer, versus going with a friend. When you have a trainer, they create routines for you, they count your reps, they motivate you. That's what a coach is doing for you in your business. They're not going to slack off. They'll help you overcome whatever challenges are in the way of your success. It's important to find the right coach for your style. It's also quite possible you'll outgrow a coach and need different support as you continue to grow your business.

Mastermind Groups

The word mastermind has been used to describe everything from an entire Facebook group, a gathering of a hundred people, sessions with a dozen participants, and small groups of four to six people. First, I'm going to describe the benefits of meeting regularly with six or fewer people.

Each participant has a "hot seat" where they share a brief update and then ask a question to the group. My preferred check-in for hot seats is the "Rose, Thorn, Bud" exercise where each participant shares a win, a challenge, and something to which they're looking forward.[1] This format provides more time for updates, which allows a small group to get to know each other quickly.

Another option to consider is joining a professionally facilitated mastermind with eight to twelve participants. In this format, focus is not on individual hot seats. Each participant is encouraged to bring a question to the group each session. The coach facilitates the conversation, weaving between questions and asking for feedback from participants.

The benefit of this format is less time spent on updates and more time on questions—plus participants have access to more points of view and different ideas. It's an excellent way to broaden your network as you get to know this group of participants over time. Scheduling one-on-one calls with participants will allow you to deepen your connection.

Masterminds are similar to having accountability partners, but the group gets to know you over time. Their collective feedback and support will move you past any challenges you may be facing. Group members are also great at holding up a mirror for you to see for yourself how you're getting in your own way. Because you've built a relationship over time, members will push you to get outside your comfort zone.

Each time you meet, you'll bring your challenges to the group and invite their input. While members may not be content experts and this may not be coaching per se, you won't be let off the hook easily.

Unlike coaching, you can have a mastermind without a paid facilitator. These are peer masterminds. To be honest, your mileage may vary. When no one is paying, the commitment to attending and staying on topic wanes. It only takes one person slacking to make the entire group feel like it's not worth their time. Slowly, more members then show signs that they're no longer invested in the group.

It all depends on how the group was brought together. Did you know the members of the group before joining, or were you randomly assigned based on the fact that you were sitting together at a conference breakout session?

Occasionally, the right mix of people is brought together and co-creates a strong group that meets the needs of its members. For this to occur, usually one member takes the lead in facilitating and managing group dynamics. It's still a peer group, but it's being run as if it was a professional mastermind.

The frequency of meetings is another variable for success. This can range from every two weeks to quarterly, with monthly being the most common choice for peer masterminds.

A paid mastermind is similar to what I've described with a few key differences:

- Curation
- Facilitation
- Consistency

Professionally managed masterminds are curated, so you're more likely to be in a group with people overcoming similar challenges. If this wasn't the case, you could find yourself in a group with someone consistently earning $350,000, while someone else is trying to break past $100,000. The challenges and resources to achieve $500,000 a year are very different from those for someone at the beginning stages of their business. Curation, therefore, is key.

Conversation in a group can easily go sideways and get completely off-track. Having a coach facilitate makes it easier for everyone to participate and stay on topic. A facilitator will also notice if one member is quieter than usual or appears to be upset in some way. Ignoring these cues leads to disconnection in a group, but a facilitator can catch these issues as they occur and help bring the group back together.

Last, but certainly not least, is the concept of consistency. Many peer masterminds start off with a regular schedule, but over time their meetings become more erratic, and attendance becomes inconsistent. When a mastermind group is professionally managed, there's a fee to participate which helps all members prioritize participation. The coach or facilitator is responsible for making sure meetings are scheduled on a consistent basis.

The cost to participate in a well-curated, professionally facilitated, consistent, small group mastermind varies depending on the expertise of the person managing the group. Generally, expect to pay a few thousand dollars for a six-month program and upwards of tens of thousands of dollars for a high-end year-long mastermind.

Personal Board of Directors

I first learned about this concept in Dorie Clark's first book, *Reinventing You: Define Your Brand, Imagine Your Future.* In its simplest form, this is about mentorship: The difference is in the execution. Rather than looking for one person who's older and wiser to mentor you, broaden your search to find a variety of people who will help you realize your ideal future self. That puts less pressure to find or be the perfect mentor. There are four types of people you might include in this group:

1. **Supporters**: People who believe in you and who are fans of your work. You can trust their intent and know their feedback will be delivered with kindness.
2. **Advocates** — Experts in your field or industry who can speak up on your behalf when external validation will help your business succeed.
3. **Critics:** Include at least one loving critic who has your best interests at heart but will be brutally honest with you and tell you what they really think.[2]
4. **Detractors:** To grow beyond your limits, include one detractor. These are difficult conversations because these people have a less-than-rosy perception of you. They may not believe you will succeed. Use their criticism as

fuel to succeed beyond their limited expectations.[3]

The benefit is that you'll have a group of people to seek advice about your business. It's a bit of a misnomer to call this a board, as there are no formal meetings and no need to even inform each person of their status as a board member.

When choosing whom to include, think outside the box. Don't limit your search to more experienced professionals in your field or industry. Former clients and people who used to report to you could be sources of inspiration and provide the resources you need on your business journey. Choose people who have more experience in the areas in which you're seeking to grow.

There are no rules to how frequently you contact your board of directors. At any point, you might have a particular question that one of them can best answer. Keep an eye out for opportunities to provide support and value to this group of people. Making a mutually desired introduction, recommending their book or podcast, or referring prospective clients are all ways to show your appreciation for their ongoing support.

There really is no replacement for having a strong team of advisors backing you on your business journey. Make the effort to build and nurture your personal board of directors and you'll quickly see dividends for the time you've invested.

PART SIX: CONCLUSION

The COVID-19 pandemic impacted all of us. In my case, when my skills as a networking expert became moot, I put on my business growth strategist hat. Using a mix of experience and intuition, I tested out ways to reinvent my business. The result was I reinvented myself as a sought-after virtual event design consultant and executive Zoom producer.

By November 2020, I'd built a thriving six-figure business based on all new revenue streams, including running *The 5% Advantage Program*, which certifies Virtual Event Professionals. I also began helping national and statewide organizations strategically bring their events online with less stress and greater participant engagement.

By August 2021, I had already more than doubled my 2020 revenue and achieved the dream of homeownership—despite real estate being a seller's market.

Starting over was daunting, but I knew it was possible. I knew my strong network would provide the resources and support I needed. I had cultivated my network for years, literally and figuratively giving rides to the airport. While I didn't do it because I expected to ever need something in return, I knew they'd come through when I needed them.

Your network is an insurance policy. You pay for insurance each month hoping to never need it but knowing it will be there should catastrophe strike. Jordan Harbinger made this analogy when I interviewed him on my podcast *On the Schmooze*.[1]

While my story is about the pandemic, you never know what the reason might be you need to start over. Jordan experienced this in 2018—no pandemic or recession in sight.

For over a decade, Jordan co-hosted *Art of Charm*, a top 50 iTunes podcast, achieving almost four million downloads a month during its prime. Then he and his business partner had a falling out and Jordan lost everything. He started over with a new training company and a new podcast aptly named *The Jordan Harbinger Show*. Within ninety days, this new podcast quickly had more downloads per month than his previous show.[2]

That was possible because Jordan had been habitually networking throughout that decade. He built the well before he knew he would be thirsty. When he was at the top of his game and thinking about how to support his network, it never occurred to him that he might need their support one day to start over from scratch.

In 2020, entrepreneurs all over the globe experienced this first-hand. The businesses we had spent years and even decades building were no longer what clients needed. The entrepreneurs who were nimble and willing to try new strategies had the greatest potential of regaining their previous revenue or even surpassing it.

I shared my business journey throughout the pandemic with my network in real-time. This led to dozens of requests for coffee chats to "pick my brain." I used those chats as an opportunity to do research calls and discover what small "p" problems these entrepreneurs were finding most challenging.

Once I had an inkling of their needs, I refocused my energy around publishing this book. I'd started drafting this book in 2018 and then set it aside because the timing didn't feel right. While writing this book in 2018, I had hosted several free masterclasses on these topics to share knowledge and also learn what questions kept coming up that I needed to address.

Over the last three years, I've worked with dozens of entrepreneurs as they sought out their market to co-create their offer. Having experienced the benefits of these best practices firsthand, I knew it was time to share them with a wider audience.

In 2021, when the book was nearly ready to launch, I hosted a series of *Pop-Up Masterminds*. Over sixty entrepreneurs tested out the *Wake Up Your Network* exercise in this book because it was the pre-work for those sessions.

Based on the feedback I experienced thus far, I realized there was an opportunity to create a group program. One-on-one coaching meets the needs of some clients, but several likely prospects indicated they would appreciate being in a community or group while they worked through the steps outlined in the book. The additional insights and accountability from group members would help them keep moving towards achieving their business goals.

That's how I decided to launch the Wake Up Your Network Program,[3] which offers a mix of mastermind sessions and one-on-one coaching calls to help you implement the strategies in this book.

The program promise or outcome you will achieve if you do the work is:

You will stop struggling to find an audience for your offers because you'll co-create an offer they can't resist. You'll be adept at implementing a repeatable process that helps you discover likely prospects from within your existing network who already know, like, and trust you.

While you may not achieve the same results as quickly, my story demonstrates that building on over a decade of experience, it's possible to develop new programs, establish credibility in a new area, and deliver tremendous value.

As a business growth strategist, I coach entrepreneurs on how to go from an idea to product/market fit and to develop strategies for lead generation and sales conversions.

To avoid building an offer no one wants to buy, I help them assess their network to discover likely prospects and referral partners and provide best practices for engaging with those connections through target market research and program pilots.

Throughout this book, I've shared specific strategies for creating powerful offers for your clients. I can't wait to hear the result you've achieved by following the steps I've outlined. I'd love to hear what resonates with you in this book and how you were inspired to take action. Email action@SmallListBigResults.com to share the big results you attain by taking these actions.

NOTES

Part One: Mindset

1. Gill Corkindale, "Overcoming Imposter Syndrome," *Harvard Business Review*, May 7, 2008, https://hbr.org/2008/05/overcoming-imposter-syndrome.
2. "Dorie Clark: Official Website," Dorie Clark, accessed September 26, 2021, http://www.dorieclark.com.
3. Robbie Samuels, "When Will Women Win the Right to Pockets?" August 11, 2015, https://robbiesamuels.com/when-will-women-win-the-right-to-pockets.
4. Robbie Samuels, "OTS 002: When Will Women Win the Right to Pockets—Robbie Samuels," *On the Schmooze*, Podcast audio, July 18, 2016, https://robbiesamuels.com/ots-002-when-will-women-win-the-right-to-pockets-robbie-samuels.
5. Dorie Clark, *Stand Out: How to Find Your Breakthrough Idea and Build a Following Around It* (New York: Portfolio, 2015), http://www.dorieclark.com/stand-out.
6. *On the Schmooze*, Podcast, Robbie Samuels, www.OntheSchmooze.com.
7. Robbie Samuels, *Croissants vs. Bagels: Strategic, Effective, and Inclusive Networking at Conferences* (Movement Publishing: 2017), http://www.CroissantsvsBagels.com.
8. W Chan Kim and Renée Mauborgne, *Blue Ocean Strategy: How to Create Uncontested Market Space and Make the Competition Irrelevant* (Boston: Harvard Business School Press, 2015).
9. Jonathan Acuff, *Finish: Give Yourself the Gift of Done* (New York: Portfolio/Penguin, 2018).

Part Two: Stacking Your Successes

1. *Smart Passive Income with Pat Flynn*, accessed September 26, 2021, https://www.smartpassiveincome.com/shows/spi.
2. "Homepage," n.d., Jason van Orden, accessed September 26, 2021, https://jasonvanorden.com.
3. "SPI 100: A Look Back with Two People Who Changed My Life Forever," n.d., *Smart Passive Income*, accessed September 26, 2021,

https://www.smartpassiveincome.com/podcasts/episode-100-a-look-back.
4. *Impact: How to Grow Your Thought Leadership Brand and Business*, accessed September 26, 2021, https://podcasts.apple.com/us/podcast/impact-how-to-grow-your-thought-leadership-brand-and/id1497476974.
5. "Finding and Acting on Your Passion with Jason Van Orden," *Hired By Passion Podcast*, April 2, 2020, https://music.amazon.com/podcasts/298bda04-33e9-4e04-861f-58d9bd050c5e/episodes/a8a7ab0c-cc5a-4d58-ba16-66ca4d3ca864/hired-by-passion-podcast-finding-and-acting-on-your-passion-with-jason-van-orden.
6. "76 Top Michael Chabon Quotes That Give Insight into Life," n.d., *The Famous People*, accessed September 26, 2021, https://quotes.thefamouspeople.com/michael-chabon-2348.php.
7. "Sensible Woo | Woo Is the New You," n.d., accessed September 26, 2021, https://www.sensiblewoo.com/.

Part Three: Engage Your Network

1. "9 Ways to Network in a Pandemic," n.d., *Robbie Samuels*, accessed September 26, 2021, http://www.robbiesamuels.com/9ways.
2. "Recognized Expert." n.d., Dorie Clark Courses, accessed September 26, 2021, http://www.dorieclark.com/rex.
3. "#NoMoreBadZoom Virtual Happy Hours," n.d., *Robbie Samuels*, accessed September 26, 2021, http://www.NoMoreBadZoom.com.
4. Clark, "Recognized Expert."
5. Eugene M. Schwartz, *Breakthrough Advertising: How to Write Ads That Shatter Traditions and Sales Records* (Prentice-Hall, 1966), https://amzn.to/3Eiv5Yi.
6. "Mirasee | Reimagine Business," n.d., accessed September 26, 2021, http://www.mirasee.com.
7. "Homepage," n.d., Jason van Orden, accessed September 26, 2021, http://www.jasonvanorden.com.
8. "Enabling or Disabling Closed Captioning and Live Transcription Services," n.d., Zoom Help Center, accessed September 26, 2021, https://support.zoom.us/hc/en-us/articles/4409683389709.
9. "Coaching & Mastermind," n.d., Robbie Samuels, accessed September 26, 2021, http://www.robbiesamuels.com/mastermind.

Part Four: Taking the Leap

1. *The Sun*, "Bear Cub Climbs Mountain to Reunite with Mama Bear," n.d., YouTube, accessed September 26, 2021, https://www.youtube.com/watch?v=rhjBXnEFKQs.
2. "Denise Jacobs: Speaker + Author + Creativity Evangelist," n.d., Denise Jacobs, accessed September 26, 2021, https://denisejacobs.com.
3. Denise Jacobs, *LinkedIn*, accessed September 26, 2021, https://www.linkedin.com/learning/instructors/denise-jacobs.
4. Dorie Clark, *LinkedIn*, accessed September 26, 2021, https://www.linkedin.com/learning/instructors/dorie-clark.
5. "Jim Rohn," n.d., Jim Rohn Blog, accessed September 26, 2021, http://www.jimrohn.com.
6. David Burkus, *Friend of a Friend: Understanding the Hidden Networks That Can Transform Your Life and Your Career* (Boston: Houghton Mifflin Harcourt, 2018).
7. W Chan Kim and Renée Mauborgne, *Blue Ocean Strategy: How to Create Uncontested Market Space and Make the Competition Irrelevant* (Boston: Harvard Business School Press, 2015).
8. John David Mann and Bob Burg, *The Go-Giver, Expanded Edition: A Little Story about a Powerful Business Idea* (New York: Portfolio, 2015).

Part Five: Getting Support

1. Digital Pilgrim, "Rose, Thorn, Bud," *Design Thinking Out of the Box*, July 21, 2018, https://designthinkingoutofthebox.com/2018/07/21/the-journey-begins.
2. Tasha Eurich, *Insight: The Surprising Truth about How Others See Us, How We See Ourselves, and Why the Answers Matter More than We Think* (New York: Currency, 2018).
3. Sabina Nawaz, "To Get Promoted, Get Feedback from Your Critics," *Harvard Business Review*, November 10, 2016, https://hbr.org/2016/11/to-get-promoted-get-feedback-from-your-critics.

Part Six: Conclusion

1. Samuels, Robbie, "OTS 094: Habitual Networking - Jordan Harbinger," *On the Schmooze*, May 15, 2018, https://robbiesamuels.com/ots-094-habitual-networking-jordan-harbinger.

2. "Jordan Harbinger Leaves Art of Charm," n.d., *Jordan Harbinger*, accessed September 26, 2021, https://www.jordanharbinger.com/jordan-harbinger-leaves-art-of-charm.
3. "Wake Up Your Network Program," n.d., Robbie Samuels, accessed September 26, 2021, http://www.robbiesamuels.com/mastermind.

ACKNOWLEDGMENTS

In 2017, I published my first book, *Croissants vs. Bagels: Strategic, Effective, and Inclusive Networking at Conferences*. I knew I wanted it to be a launching pad for creating group programs but I didn't yet have a clear sense of my target market. The book had a very successful launch—it reached #1 in three Amazon categories and received 150 Amazon reviews within a week. The big question was how to capitalize on this momentum.

Following in the footsteps of my friend and mentor, Dorie Clark, who had just launched her Recognized Expert course, I decided to test a pilot program. Not knowing what I know now, I skipped a few steps and made the usual first-time errors—creating the pilot in a vacuum without any input from likely prospects. Despite my clumsy efforts, I did get a pilot off the ground—and as Dorie prophesied, I learned a lot.

Special thanks to the clients who joined me for the pilot and first iteration of my coaching program: Jennifer

Fondrevay, Pam Garramone, Lisa Goldstein, Tammy Gooler Loeb, Sarah Kohl, Jenny Lisk, and Gina Warner. Without their encouragement, I would not have realized I was onto something.

The journey from pilot to the first iteration was fraught. Fortunately, around that time, I had the opportunity to meet with business strategist Marilee Driscoll. I had started to pay attention to who was attracted to me and to my work—and I realized it was predominantly entrepreneurial women in their 50s. That led to a complete rebranding of the program, which became The M.O.R.E. Program for Entrepreneurial Women.

As my business grew, so did my questions. I've had the good fortune of having amazing peer support over the years. I've met regularly with Tony Chatman, Stacey Copas, Charlene DeCesare, Denise Jacobs, Rachel Sheerin, and Kali Williams. Shout out to Dorie Clark, her Trajectory Mastermind members, and members of her Recognized Expert community. Gratitude to Michael Roderick and his G.A.T.E. community.

It's hard to overstate how my network supported me as I reinvented myself in 2020. My free weekly #NoMoreBadZoom Virtual Happy Hour has thrived since March 13, 2020, because of the support of regular attendees: Amber Browning-Coyle, Regina Carey, Scott Dell, David Fox, Kathleen Graffunder, Dorita Hatchett, Annie Hopson, Gayle Lantz, Annette Mason, Erika Salloux, Rachel Wagner, Dorothy Wilhelm, Lynne Williams—and dozens of others who have attended this weekly event over thirty times in the last eighteen months.

I launched The 5% Advantage Program in May 2020 because my network trusted me to teach them how to create engaging virtual presentations. I'm especially pleased this led to hiring some of the members I certified as virtual event professionals, including Christopher Johnson, Jen Bonardi, and Nicole Oullette, to support my event clients.

Speaking of event clients, I wouldn't have any if I wasn't given a chance early on by the Association of Talent & Development Southern Connecticut chapter and the California Notary Symposium. That led to regularly supporting the virtual events of such amazing mission-driven organizations like the California WIC Association, Feeding America, and the Visiting Nurse Service of New York.

While this reinvention was taking hold, I was also working with the team at Mirasee coaching entrepreneurs on their journey towards greater impact and income. It was an honor to support these entrepreneurs and receive support in my growth as a business growth strategy coach. Special thanks to Lisa Bloom, Joey Gourdji, Ari Iny, Danny Iny, Amber Kinney, Tonya Kubo, Bhoomi Pathak, Mary Williams, and Jim Wright.

Mary Williams subsequently became my systems and processes business coach, helping me "adult" my business as it quickly grew into a thriving six-figure company. Along for this entire journey, starting in February 2020 and not knowing what she was saying yes to, is Peya Robbins. Peya is my virtual assistant, and she's worked hard to adapt to the ever-evolving and changing needs of my business.

My world would be incomplete without my wife, Jess Samuels. She married me knowing I was entrepreneurial and believed I could create a successful business. With her unyielding support, ten years later, I finally became an "overnight success" and was able to buy our dream home for our family.

And last but not least, thank you as a whole to my Launch Team members–over 500 people signed up to help make this book a huge success. Your support means the world to me!

ABOUT THE AUTHOR

Robbie Samuels is an author, speaker, and business growth strategy coach who has been recognized as a networking expert by *Harvard Business Review*, *Forbes*, *Lifehacker*, and *Inc*. He is also a virtual event design consultant and executive Zoom producer. He has been recognized as an industry expert in the field of digital event design by JDC Events.

Robbie is the author of *Croissants vs. Bagels: Strategic, Effective, and Inclusive Networking at Conferences* and has been profiled in *Harvard Business Review*, *Forbes*, and *Fast Company*. He is a *Harvard Business Review* contributor.

His clients include entrepreneurs, thought leaders, associations, national and statewide advocacy organizations, women's leadership summits, and corporations, including Feeding America, California WIC Association, Marriott, AmeriCorps, and Hostelling International.

Robbie is the host of the *On the Schmooze* podcast and #NoMoreBadZoom Virtual Happy Hours. He resides in the Philadelphia area with his wife and two children. Learn more about him and his work: www.robbiesamuels.com.

A REQUEST

THANK YOU for Reading My Book!

I would love to hear from you. Writing an Amazon review (www.robbiesamuels.com/review) is as easy as answering any of these questions:

- What did you enjoy about the book?
- What is your most valuable takeaway or insight?
- What have you done differently—or what will you do differently—because of what you read?
- To whom would you recommend this book?

Seriously, just two or three sentences would be amazing. Your feedback helps to get this book into the hands of those who need it most.

I look forward to hearing about the action you took because of this book.

Thank you in advance,
Robbie

Download the Big Results Toolkit (for FREE)!

READ THIS

To help you implement the strategies in this book, I've created several resources, including the *Wake Up Your Network* workbook. Download them all at no cost whatsoever in the Big Results Toolkit. It's my gift to you. - *Robbie Samuels*

Go to www.robbiesamuels.com/toolkit to get it!

www.ingramcontent.com/pod-product-compliance
Lightning Source LLC
LaVergne TN
LVHW061616070526
838199LV00078B/7308